Wisconsin Indians

Revised and Expanded Edition

Nancy Oestreich Lurie

Curator Emerita
Milwaukee Public Museum

THE WISCONSIN HISTORICAL SOCIETY PRESS

Madison

Published by Wisconsin Historical Society Press

© 2002 by the State Historical Society of Wisconsin

Photographs identified with PH, WHi, or WHS are from the Society's
collections; address inquiries about such photos to the Visual Materials
Archivist, at the above address.

Publications of the Wisconsin Historical Society are available at quantity
discounts for promotions, fund raising, and educational use. Write to the above
address for more information.

Printed in the United States of America
Designed by Jane Tenenbaum
Maps on pages 6 and 7 by Amelia Janes/Mike Gallagher, Midwest Educational Graphics
Cover photo courtesy of Jackson County Historical Society —
Van Schaick Collection

06 05 04   5 4 3 2

Library of Congress Cataloging-in-Publication Data
Lurie, Nancy Oestreich.
    Wisconsin Indians / Nancy Oestreich Lurie; foreword by Francis Paul
Prucha. Rev. and expanded 2nd ed.
        p. cm.
    Includes bibliographical references.
    ISBN 0-87020-330-4
        1. Indians of North America — Wisconsin — History. 2. Indians of
North America — Wisconsin — Governmental relations. I. Title.

E78.W8 L87 2002
977.5'00497-dc21
                                                            2001049757

CONTENTS

The original Great Seal of the Territory of Wisconsin, created in 1839, included the motto "Civilization takes the place of barbarism." Notice the strong suggestion of Indians being pushed west across the Mississippi River. This design, with minor modifications, was also used after Wisconsin gained statehood in 1848; the seal was redesigned in 1851 and again in 1881.

FOREWORD

by Francis Paul Prucha, S. J.

American Indians, descendants of the aboriginal peoples who inhab-ited the North American continent before the invasion of the Euro-peans, have always been a significant part of the history of the United States. At times, to be sure, they almost disappeared from the conscious-ness of America's dominant white society, but on other occasions, spe-cial events and special concerns have thrust them into the spotlight.

During the Revolutionary War period, Indians played a part as al-lies or enemies of the new republic. In the 1820s and 1830s they gained attention because of Indian policy associated with President Andrew Jackson, which moved large numbers of Indians from the East and set-tled them west of the Mississippi River. After the Civil War, spectacular Indian wars in the West led to a "peace" initiative, which aimed to locate the tribes on reservations and then to assimilate the Indians by dividing the reservation lands into allotments for individual families. In the twen-tieth century, Indians came into public view again as Commissioner of Indian Affairs John Collier in the 1930s overturned assimilationist poli-cies by restoring Indian tribal cultures and the tribes' political autonomy.

The last decades of the twentieth century, however, have been the most exciting and noteworthy period for Indian tribes and their rela-tionship to the dominant society. After a brief setback in the 1950s, the movement toward self-determination that began under Collier ad-vanced steadily during the 1960s, reached a high point in the 1970s, and has continued up to the present time.

Yet many people, unfortunately, still see Indians in a romantic light. The universally recognized symbols of Indians all come out of the past — bows and arrows, tomahawks, smoke signals, peace pipes, feathered headdresses, and tepees. But the remnants of an earlier material culture should not obscure the reality of the Indian existence in the present. Self-determination and self-governance are now official federal policy, so strong at times that Indians' pursuit of treaty rights has caused a backlash from some whites who argue that Indians are being given too many privileges. Indian population, too, which reached a nadir of about 237,000 in 1900, steadily increased during the twentieth century, until in 2000 the Census Bureau counted 2,476,000 persons who called themselves Indians.

Today's Americans who aren't Indians need to gain more than a passing acquaintance with the Indians in their midst. They must learn to know the tribal people who share American citizenship but who, as well, struggle to preserve their original cultural values and special legal rights.

One way to learn about Indians is to study the history of tribes in a particular state. Throughout the Indians' early history, of course, the artificial political boundaries of the states did not exist, and the anthropologists have used "culture areas" to distinguish geographically the various groups of Indians. Furthermore, in United States national history, the Indians fall under federal, not state, jurisdiction. Yet states have come to play an important part in Indian affairs, and all non-Indian citizens of a state should learn about the Indians who live among them. Through that knowledge they can move toward an understanding of federal Indian policies and programs in general. Many historians of Indian affairs in the United States tend, logically enough, to study Indian policies first at the national level and then look to see how those policies have been implemented at a local or state level. But Indian affairs can also be read in the reverse order by studying first what happened at the state and local levels to discover what federal policy has been.

Nancy Oestreich Lurie's new edition of *Wisconsin Indians,* like its predecessors published in 1969 and 1980, is a unique book about Indians of a single state. An anthropologist — and one with strong historical interests — Lurie has spent her career in close contact with the Indians of Wisconsin. She knows about the past of the seven tribes now residing in the state and recounts their history succinctly in this book. She notes that Wisconsin, again and again, has been a natural laboratory for government policies, so much so that Wisconsin becomes, in her words, "an astonishingly representative illustration of the historical development of federal Indian policy and Indian reaction to it." Still, she does not intend to present a full-blown history of federal Indian affairs, even as acted out in Wisconsin, but instead to call attention to certain aspects of policies and programs that impinged in important ways on the Indians of the state and therefore on all its citizens. Her emphasis is on recent developments and on the present status of the Indians.

Lurie's tone is conversational rather than didactic, and she is fully sensitive to Indian viewpoints, which she has absorbed from personal contacts and from tribal newspapers and Web sites. She furnishes valuable insights into Indian matters. Especially instructive are her accounts of Menominee termination and tribal restoration, the fishing rights controversy of the Chippewas, the conflict about mining in Forest County, the development of an Indian school in Milwaukee, and the successful bingo and casino operations — all of which have national as well as local significance.

Nancy Lurie's Wisconsin Indians do not fit the stereotype of Indians living a simple life in a romantic and distant past. They are complex human communities that are fully alive today, changing and adapting to the world around them without losing entirely the spiritual and cultural traits that give them their distinctive character.

I wrote, some years ago, in urging readers to take an interest in Indians, "The Indians, once facilely thought to be a vanishing race as a result of disappearance into the dominant white society, are instead persistent and clearly identifiable groups within the nation, whose history it behooves us all to know, and whose rights and dignity it becomes us all to respect." *Wisconsin Indians* will help make that possible.

PREFACE TO THE 2002 EDITION

In 1969, when the first version of this publication appeared, I hoped it would answer frequently asked questions and correct common misunderstandings about American Indians in regard to the history and effects of federal Indian policy. It was obvious as early as 1961 that there was a new ferment among Indian people to secure their legal and political rights and gain greater control of their community affairs. When I updated this publication in 1980, I noted how the tribes were creating new tactics to deal with old problems, in turn stimulating new reactions on the part of non-Indians to pose further challenges for Indian people.

My description of events that unfolded between 1969 and 1980 depended in large part on the file of newspaper clippings about American Indians at the Milwaukee Public Museum anthropology department, my own observations and unpublished notes, and personal communication with knowledgeable individuals among the Wisconsin tribes, local and national Indian organizations, and various offices in the Bureau of Indian Affairs (BIA). This remains true for much of the information covered since 1980, but new research included much greater recourse to tribal and national Indian newspapers. These have an old, if sporadic, history but proliferated rapidly in Wisconsin as elsewhere by the 1970s. This edition also takes extensive advantage of the fact that Indian people availed themselves enthusiastically of the electronic media almost as soon as it was generally available in the 1980s, creating and regularly updating tribal and pan-Indian interest groups' Web sites to educate the general public about Indian matters and to communicate among themselves to further their own interests.

As was the case in 1969, Wisconsin continues to offer an unusual opportunity to understand the national Indian picture. Over the years the state has served as a kind of natural laboratory for most of the government's policies and programs, while at the same time Wisconsin Indian tribes and organizations have exemplified and sometimes led in new developments to improve the lives of Indian people. My objective to

provide a parsimonious framework for further study of historic and contemporary Indian life and understand Indian news as it occurs has become increasingly difficult. The accelerated pace and expanding scope
of Indian affairs required some hard decisions about what to include
and what to drop or condense from the 1980 publication.

In this edition, I think it is necessary to discuss two terms at the outset insofar as they have figured prominently in recent years. These are
tribe and *Native American*. *Tribe* is used in two ways that I believe can be
readily distinguished by the contexts in which they occur. Without getting into academic debates over levels of complexity, anthropologically
speaking for the world at large, *tribe* stands for a group whose members
recognize common kinship, customs, and principles of social organization that distinguish them from other such groups. Tribes provide stabil-
ity for people to survive, but they are not static. Bands can break off and
retain their sense of tribal identity despite a good deal of local autonomy and adaptation to different challenges or opportunities, or they can
become so separated by time and distance that they become new tribes.
New tribes can develop out of coalitions or alliances or can be reconsti-
tuted out of the remnants of former tribes.

Bureaucratically speaking, that is, on a national level according to
the Bureau of Indian Affairs (BIA), a separately budgeted and adminis-
tered unit is considered a tribe even though its official name might be as
a band, nation, pueblo, rancheria, or whatever, because its membership
is confined to its own "tribal roll." The Potawatomi, for example, are descendants of the anthropological Potawatomi tribe, but each of the
present Potawatomi administrative units in Kansas, Oklahoma, Wisconsin, and Michigan has its own Tribal Roll. All four are counted separately among the more than five hundred "tribes" the BIA serves.
Potawatomi enclaves in Canada, where Indian groups are called
"bands" and live on "reserves," are also descendants of the anthropological tribe but don't even exist as far as the BIA is concerned.

A note is in order here regarding terminology applied to the hierar-
chy of authority in the administration of Indian affairs over time. The
governor of a territory also was the superintendent of Indian affairs in
the territory, with regional agents to do much of the work of dealing
with tribes. With statehood and settlement of the tribes on reservations,
the term *superintendent* referred to regional administrators, with agents
serving local reservations where one or more tribes might be resident.

After 1900, reservation school superintendents took the place of agents, and the term *superintendent* was then applied to the person in charge of a tribe or reservation.

As to *Native American*, it is *not* more politically correct than *American Indian*, although the media seems bent on making everyone think it is. I don't use it very often except to cite the titles of some organizations. The term was first promoted to whites in the early twentieth century with the official chartering of the Native American Church (NAC) in response to government and missionary opposition and misrepresentations that this new pan-Indian religious movement was an evil, orgiastic pagan cult. In reality, the NAC is a Bible-based fundamentalist Christian faith that uses peyote as a sacrament combined with Indian symbols and ritual practices.

The term *Native American* gained much wider, though brief, currency during the early stages of the Indian rights movement of the 1970s, as it supposedly pointed out and corrected Columbus's geographical stupidity. By the time non-Indians embraced the term, it was no longer very popular among Indian people, and it had not been universally adopted by them in the first place. An important legacy of the period, the Native American Rights Fund (NARF), which provides legal assistance, has not abandoned the term *American Indian;* in fact, that term is necessary to distinguish these Native American clients from other Native Americans: Hawaiians, Samoans, Guamanians, and Eskimos (*Inuit* is the preferred term in Canada, where the collective term for Indians and Inuit is simply *natives,* or, more recently, "First Nations"). Apart from NAC members, for most Indian people it is a matter of indifference which term non-Indians use, and at this time they say "Indian" or "Indian people" considerably more often than "Native American." When particular tribes are meant, there is overwhelming preference for their own names, which are not necessarily the names by which they are known to the general public. People who really want to be politically correct should learn these names.

To me, the almost self-righteous use of the term *Native American* instead of *Indian* on the part of well-meaning but uninformed non-Indians is just the latest evidence of how ingrained the assumption is that the Indians must inevitably assimilate. Now that it is acceptable in mainstream America to celebrate ancestral ethnicity, Indians can be different just like everybody else — German Americans, Irish Americans, Italian

Americans, African Americans. . . . In my mind's ear I still hear the late Josie Daniels, an elder from the Forest County Potawatomi Reservation, speaking to an audience of white college students in Milwaukee some thirty years ago: "This is our 'Old Country.' If we lose what makes us who we are, there is no place we can go to find it again."

In discussing the various tribes, the following names will be used. *Chippewa* appended to reservation names — Bad River, Lac Courte Oreilles — remains the acceptable official name although the variant form, *Ojibwa* (both words variously spelled), is found in nongovernmental publications. There is disagreement on what it means and where it came from, but it isn't offensive. The people refer to themselves as *Anishinabe* (ahnishinahbee), "friends" or "the people." It is fairly common throughout North America that a people's own name simply means "people," whereas outsiders are designated by special names. For this reason, many tribes are known by names other tribes had given them in response to questions from early Europeans' questions about neighboring tribes. Such is the case with *Winnebago*, probably of Menominee or Chippewa derivation, rendered *Puant* by the French and translated into English as *Stinkard*, supposedly because of the marshes where they lived on Green Bay. They call themselves *Ho-Chunk*, meaning "Big Voice" or "original speech," in reference to their primacy among their linguistically closest relatives, the Iowa, Oto, and Missouria. In 1994 they officially changed their name from the Winnebago Tribe of Wisconsin to the Ho-Chunk Nation. I reluctantly retain the use of Winnebago as it occurs in virtually all historical references until the Ho-Chunk Nation (HCN, their own abbreviation) began generating publications themselves since 1994, and thenceforth I use Ho-Chunk.

Menominee and *Potawatomi* are used as reasonable approximations to their own names meaning, respectively, "Wild Rice People" and "Keepers of the Fire." The same is true of *Oneida*, "the People of the Standing Stone." The Stockbridge-Munsee and Brothertown tribes are descendants of a number of eastern seaboard tribes who constituted themselves as new tribes under these names.

❧ ❧

It is not possible to list all the people who helped me in preparing *Wisconsin Indians*, but I do want to express my sincere thanks and acknowledge my debt of gratitude. I am particularly grateful to readers who caught errors in the 1980 publication, which I have corrected in this edition. Any remaining or new errors of fact or interpretation are mine alone. Finally, usage varies whether to say "Menominees" or "Menominee," for example. I have made an arbitrary decision to use s̲ to indicate plural.

❧ 1 ❧

OVERVIEW

The boundaries of the state of Wisconsin encompass an astonishingly representative illustration of the historical development of federal Indian policy and Indian reaction to it. Wisconsin's Indian population of more than 50,000 people (as estimated from tribal enrollments, the 2000 census, and other sources) is the fourth largest east of the Mississippi River. North Carolina, Florida, and New York have more Indian residents, but Wisconsin includes a greater variety of tribal and linguistic proveniences and administrative complications. Many western states have much larger Indian populations, but only a few — notably Alaska, Arizona, California, New Mexico, and Oklahoma — offer more diversity than Wisconsin's three major linguistic stocks, seven broad tribal affiliations, and twelve federally recognized Indian communities covering just about the whole range of experiments in Indian policy, from the founding of the republic to the present day.

By the 1980s, in Wisconsin as elsewhere, half or more of the people had moved from their tribal communities to urban areas, where Indian social and self-help organizations assist newcomers in adjusting to city life. Although Indian people live in Green Bay, Madison, and other cities, the state's largest intertribal urban population is in Milwaukee (variously estimated today at around 10,000), where Indian people began settling in the 1920s and, in 1937, founded the state's first (and among the nation's oldest) urban Indian organizations, the Consolidated Tribes of Milwaukee. It was supplanted gradually during the 1970s by other organizations, now numbering about two dozen, that took over and expanded on its largely social functions to serve Indian people in regard to employment, health, education, housing, general welfare, and recreation. Although most of the Indian residents in Milwaukee come from Wisconsin tribes, members of tribes from many parts of the country also live in Milwaukee. Similarly, members of Wisconsin tribes can be found in other cities across the nation.

Because they were generally lost to view in the cities, urban Indians have often been considered by the public at large and even by the BIA as "assimilated," but such is not really the case. Although there is regular "spin-off" of a small percentage of Indian people into the American mainstream, "city Indians" generally maintain their tribal affiliations and identity as Indians. Since the 1960s they have made their presence and special concerns, both in the cities and on the reservations, increasingly visible. Traditionally they tend to be visitors and "commuters," exploiting urban economic opportunities without the same sense of commitment of other Americans, black and white, to an irreversible transition to urbanism. Even longtime city residents keep their family and tribal ties with regular visits home and look forward to returning to "the rez'" when they retire. The automobile, telephone, tape recorder, and now the computer are part of contemporary Indian culture — just as that other European import, the horse, was incorporated into Indian culture on the Indians' terms a few centuries ago.

All this should not be surprising. From the time of European contact right up through the treaty period that created reservations in the nineteenth century, the indigenous people of North America were primarily hunters and gatherers. Despite huge population centers obviously based on intensive agriculture in the Southeast that were abandoned about the time of European contact for reasons that still are not fully understood, the groups north of Mexico were relatively recent food producers from the perspective of the worldwide diffusion of agriculture. Gardeners rather than farmers (and historically never peasants), they remained dependent on the hunt for animal protein and the use of many natural resources for food and other purposes. Their only domesticated animal was the dog, occasionally eaten at religious feasts but kept mainly as watchdogs and pets, though on the Plains across the Mississippi they served as pack animals. In the northern part of Wisconsin, gardening was chancy at best. The complex of semitropical plants — squash, beans, corn, and tobacco — had been adapted selectively to ever shorter growing seasons as agriculture diffused out of Mexico to the lower Mississippi Valley and reached the upper Midwest about 1000 A.D.

Archeological studies now suggest that the idea of domesticating local plants, such as sunflowers, might have occurred independently in the Ohio River Valley some time before the new crops arrived and facilitated their ready adoption.

For Indian people, survival depended on mobility, resourcefulness, and adaptability coupled with a strong sense of communal responsibility to share in lean times and times of abundance. The economics of family life were centripetal, as the anthropologist John Provinse so aptly put it, in contrast to the centrifugal nature of thoroughly agrarian households. Individually or in task groups, family members frequently moved out from settled villages or semi-permanent camps for varying periods of time to obtain resources in different locations according to season and bring them back to the homeplace. Widespread trade networks also existed to move items great distances from their places of origin.

After World War II, increasing numbers of Indian people began spending more time in cities, partly due to federal programs instituted in the 1950s to encourage relocation with the expectation it would lead to assimilation, and partly due to Indian population growth exceeding localized community resources. There often are enormous discrepancies between the number of people listed on the tribal roll and those actually resident in the tribal settlement.

Yet to understand the Indian scene and its historical antecedents, close account must be taken of the tribal homelands as fundamental social and cultural foci of Indian life. Wisconsin is an excellent test of the hypothesis that, given improved conditions on the reservations, people will come home. It is among the handful of states to date where various legal and environmental conditions make Indian gaming an economic success. Reservation gaming, beginning with Bingo, appeared on the national scene as an Indian idea in Florida in 1979 and spread from tribe to tribe. Provinse's commentary published in 1965 in *Human Organization*, the journal of the Society for Applied Anthropology, was almost prophetic in noting the long-standing failure of federal efforts to make the centripetal Indian people into individual settled farmers. In Provinse's opinion they were pre-adapted for entrepreneurial enterprises.

And Indian people are coming home. Gaming provides new employment opportunities and supports programs that can begin addressing old problems of substandard living conditions regarding health, housing, welfare, and education on the reservations. It is of particular interest that almost as soon as gaming began, tribes also earmarked funds for cultural activities, language programs, tribal archives and museums, and land acquisition.

❧ 2 ❧

WISCONSIN INDIAN LANDS AND PEOPLES

Tribes that are officially "recognized" (or "acknowledged") by the United States are eligible for various entitlements, usually through the Indian Bureau, including land held and protected under what is termed "federal trust." (Contemporary tribal land holdings are shown on map 1, page 6.) Although these lands are within the boundaries of Wisconsin, they are exempt from state taxation. There has been severe loss of trust lands since the nineteenth century, when those lands were supposedly guaranteed to the tribes forever. Chapter 4 details the reasons for the loss of reservation land. As shown on the map, some tribes did not receive trust lands until the twentieth century, and a few had small amounts of land restored during the 1930s. The Wisconsin tribes, like tribes elsewhere, are now engaged in acquiring land to make up, at least in some small measure, for earlier losses and are having them put under federal trust. Since these programs are in process, it is not possible to cite accurate acreages. Consult the various tribes' Web sites for updates and other information.

Chippewa communities are scattered from the St. Lawrence River in Canada across northern Michigan, Wisconsin, Minnesota, North Dakota, and Montana and over the Canadian border in Saskatchewan. This distribution reflects a westerly expansion, largely in historic times, to find new fur-trapping resources. There are six Chippewa reservations in Wisconsin. Bad River in Ashland County, Lac du Flambeau largely in Vilas County but partly in Iron County, Lac Courte Oreilles in Sawyer County, and Red Cliff in Bayfield County were established by treaty in

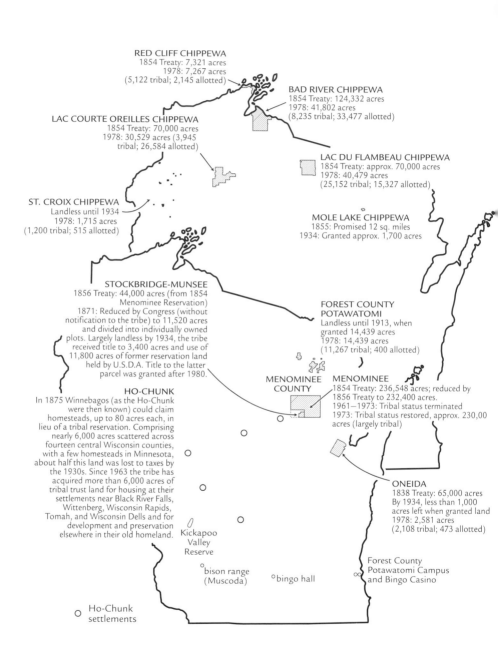

RED CLIFF CHIPPEWA
1854 Treaty: 7,321 acres
1978: 7,267 acres
(5,122 tribal; 2,145 allotted)

BAD RIVER CHIPPEWA
1854 Treaty: 124,332 acres
1978: 41,802 acres
(8,235 tribal; 33,477 allotted)

LAC COURTE OREILLES CHIPPEWA
1854 Treaty: 70,000 acres
1978: 30,529 acres (3,945
tribal; 26,584 allotted)

LAC DU FLAMBEAU CHIPPEWA
1854 Treaty: approx. 70,000 acres
1978: 40,479 acres
(25,152 tribal; 15,327 allotted)

ST. CROIX CHIPPEWA
Landless until 1934
1978: 1,715 acres
(1,200 tribal; 515 allotted)

MOLE LAKE CHIPPEWA
1855: Promised 12 sq. miles
1934: Granted approx. 1,700 acres

STOCKBRIDGE-MUNSEE
1856 Treaty: 44,000 acres (from 1854
Menominee Reservation)
1871: Reduced by Congress (without
notification to the tribe) to 11,520 acres
and divided into individually owned
plots. Largely landless by 1934, the tribe
received title to 3,400 acres and use of
11,800 acres of former reservation land
held by U.S.D.A. Title to the latter
parcel was granted after 1980.

FOREST COUNTY
POTAWATOMI
Landless until 1913, when
granted 14,439 acres
1978: 14,439 acres
(11,267 tribal; 400 allotted)

HO-CHUNK
In 1875 Winnebagos (as the Ho-Chunk
were then known) could claim
homesteads, up to 80 acres each, in
lieu of a tribal reservation. Comprising
nearly 6,000 acres scattered across
fourteen central Wisconsin counties,
with a few homesteads in Minnesota,
about half this land was lost to taxes by
the 1930s. Since 1963 the tribe has
acquired more than 6,000 acres of
tribal trust land for housing at their
settlements near Black River Falls,
Wittenberg, Wisconsin Rapids,
Tomah, and Wisconsin Dells and for
development and preservation
elsewhere in their old homeland.

MENOMINEE
COUNTY

MENOMINEE
1854 Treaty: 236,548 acres; reduced by
1856 Treaty to 232,400 acres.
1961–1973: Tribal status terminated
1973: Tribal status restored, approx. 230,00
acres (largely tribal)

ONEIDA
1838 Treaty: 65,000 acres
By 1934, less than 1,000
acres left when granted land
1978: 2,581 acres
(2,108 tribal; 473 allotted)

Kickapoo
Valley
Reserve

°bison range
(Muscoda)   °bingo hall

Forest County
Potawatomi Campus
and Bingo Casino

○ Ho-Chunk
   settlements

MAP I
WISCONSIN INDIANS

1842
CHIPPEWA

1837
CHIPPEWA

1837
SANTEE SIOUX

1836

1836

1836

1836

1831
b

a

1827

1836

1831

c d
f
e

1848

1837

1832

W I N N E B A G O

SAUK
and FOX
1804

CHIPPEWA
1816

1829

1829

OTTAWA and
POTAWATOMI

1833
CHIPPEWA,
OTTAWA
and
POTAWATOMI

Menominee   - - - - SAUK and FOX cession, 1804

MAP 2
INDIAN LAND CESSIONS

1854. Except for Red Cliff, they encompass sizeable areas: 125,000 acres at Bad River and about 75,000 acres each for the other two.

Within the boundaries of each reservation, however, there is a checkerboard of white-owned property, taxed by the state, equal to or exceeding the amount of Indian land held in tribal or individual Indian trust under the jurisdiction of the federal government. Allotted land — that is, individual trust land — usually is divided into ever smaller and scattered parcels due to inheritance by increasing numbers of descendants of the first people to receive individual trust title. Even tiny Red Cliff has lost some land, and a third of the reservation is under individual trust title. The St. Croix and Sokaogan, or Mole Lake, bands were parties to the Chippewa land cessions of 1837 and 1842 (see map 2, page 7) but were inadvertently left out of the treaty negotiations of 1854, which created reservations for four other Chippewa bands in Wisconsin. Characteristically, none of these other bands would presume to negotiate for them. The Sokaogan band somehow came to the government's attention, and in a special treaty the following year they were promised a reservation of twelve square miles, but it was never created. The St. Croix people were totally overlooked. Although their federal recognition established in earlier treaties was never cancelled, both bands lived as landless squatters. It took nearly a century for the federal government to rectify the situation, at least minimally, granting each band about 1,700 acres. At Mole Lake, an unbroken tract is under tribal trust, but the St. Croix Reservation consists of five parcels scattered over Burnett, Polk, and Barron Counties, with some 500 acres under individual trust.

The Forest County Potawatomi Reservation near the Sakoagon Chippewa consists of nearly 15,000 acres under tribal trust made up of discontinuous parcels of land stretched over some twenty miles. Like the Sakoagon Chippewa, they also had lived as squatters but as refugees from farther south. The Potawatomis' tribal estate, relinquished piecemeal in nearly fifty treaties between 1795 and 1833, had once extended roughly from the west end of Lake Erie, around the shores of Lake Michigan, and across northern Illinois to the Mississippi. In 1833, at the Treaty of Chicago, which included part of southeastern Wisconsin, the Potawatomis ceded their last land east of the Mississippi River. Most of them moved west as agreed upon by treaty; those who did not leave their homelands are referred to in old government records (with obvious exasperation) as the "strolling Potawatomis." Some stayed in Michigan and Indiana or took refuge in Canada, where they live today.

The Potawatomis who remained in Milwaukee and Waukesha Counties attracted little attention until the Sioux uprising of 1862 in Minnesota sparked a totally groundless rumor of an Indian attack that sent panicked whites fleeing for protection into Milwaukee from outlying farms and villages. It was soon apparent, to the chagrin of some people and derisive amusement of others, that there was no danger, but the incident raised questions about why the local Indians had not joined their fellow tribespeople out west. Seeing the threat of forced removal, these Potawatomis migrated northward, some going only as far as the Menominee Reservation, where they were integrated into the tribe, while the rest ended up in Forest County. The government still considered them part of the western Prairie Potawatomi band, though usually not formally enrolled, and paid no attention to them until 1913 when they were recognized as a separate tribe upon obtaining their reservation in Forest County through help from concerned whites.

Like the Chippewa bands, Potawatomi bands are spread over a wide area, but unlike the Chippewas, whose own expansion gave rise to virtually autonomous bands, the Potawatomis had a cohesive sense of tribal identity, and their dispersion into separate entities resulted from their treatment by the government. In 1847 the groups west of the Mississippi were brought together on one reservation in Kansas. Because of internal disagreements, a break-off group went to Oklahoma and was separately recognized as the Citizens Band in 1867. In Wood County, southwest of Forest County, there are a few Potawatomi families, descendants of people who began moving back from Kansas around 1900. They have no federal trust land in Wisconsin and, despite long residence here, continue to be enrolled as Prairie Potawatomis.

The Menominee Indian Reservation in east-central Wisconsin is also Menominee County, which was created for tax purposes in 1961 when the government terminated its recognition of the tribe and the federal trust status of the reservation. In 1973 the reservation and federal recognition were restored. Prior to 1961, the entire reservation of 232,400 acres was held as tribal land. It was diminished by several thousand acres during termination and now includes white-owned property as well as property owned by individual Menominees that is taxed. The tribe is currently trying to buy back property owned by non-Indians and offers Menominee land owners the option to return their land to tribal trust while continuing to reside and own any buildings on the land — the arrangement that prevailed on the reservation prior to termination. A particular distinction of the Menominees is that they are the oldest known continuous residents in Wisconsin. They also are an undivided, exclusively Wisconsin tribe, occupying a far northern portion of their original homeland. The Menominee story is an important part of the history of Indian policy and the Indian rights movement and will be taken up in detail in that context in chapter 7.

Fitting roughly into a jog in the southwest corner of the Menominee Reservation in Shawano County is the reservation of the Stockbridge-Munsee tribe. To the east, just outside of Green Bay in Brown and Outagamie Counties, is the Oneida Reservation. These two tribes and a nonreservation tribe, the Brothertown (also spelled Brotherton), often are referred to collectively in the old records as "the New York Indians." The Stockbridge and Brothertown descend from tribes of the eastern seaboard that suffered great population loss, dispersal, and sociocultural disruption during the colonial period as a result of wars and the onslaught of European diseases. They spoke Algonkian languages, the same major linguistic stock that includes Chippewa, Potawatomi, and Menominee. The Stockbridges are primarily Mohicans (or Mahicans) who originally lived along the Hudson and Connecticut River Valleys. By the mid-seventeenth century the "plantation" they held under colonial jurisdiction foreshadowed the reservation system, one of several groups of Christian converts known as "praying Indians." Though loyal to the English in King Phillip's War (1675–1676), they were frequently set upon by hostile colonists. In 1735, along with some Delawares and members of other fragmented tribes they had incorporated over time, the Mohicans formed a settlement at Stockbridge, Massachusetts. They lived much like their white neighbors, with whom they were allied in fighting against the English in the American Revolution. For all that, their settlement was overrun by non-Indians, and in 1785 they accepted the Oneidas' offer to join them in New York State.

The Brothertowns are mainly of Mohegan (distinct from Mohican, above) and Pequot descent but, like the Mohicans, included people of other tribes who took refuge among them. They originally resided in Connecticut, Rhode Island, and on Long Island. Their history of relationships with the colonists is similar to that of the Stockbridges, and they also joined the colonists against the British in the Revolutionary

War. In 1744 Samson Occom, a Mohegan Indian and ordained Presbyterian minister, formed and named the Brothertown tribe. Occom convinced seven English-speaking, Christian Indian communities to unite in central New York on land given to them by the Oneida tribe. Enclaves of some of the tribes ancestral to the Stockbridges and Brothertowns remain along the eastern seaboard.

The Oneidas are a member tribe of the famous League of the Iroquois, or Haudenosaunee. Iroquoian is a major linguistic stock, completely distinct from Algonkian. Part of the tribe, separately recognized, remains in New York State, while others moved to Canada. The League officially voted to remain neutral in the American Revolution, but some of the tribes, notably the Mohawks in Canada, fought against the Americans. Others, including the Oneidas, believed their future interests would be best served by siding with the Americans. Thus, despite differences in language between the Oneidas and the Stockbridges and Brothertowns, the three tribes were allied on political grounds. Ironically, after the Revolution all three were under increasing pressures from the Americans to give up their lands.

As early as 1818, some Stockbridges planned to settle with the Munsees, a Delaware group in Indiana, but by the time they got there the Munsees had ceded their land and joined with the Stockbridges to seek a new home. The Oneidas were divided over the issue of moving west, but one contingent led by Eleazar Williams, an Episcopal lay reader of part Indian descent, and financed by a land company eager for their New York land, negotiated with the Menominees, Winnebagos, and Chippewas in 1823 to settle with them on a stretch of land along the lower Fox River in Wisconsin. During the 1820s and 1830s, Oneida, Brothertown, and Stockbridge Indians, along with the Munsees and other refugee Delawares, moved to Wisconsin. The government tried to regularize the arrangements with a treaty in 1827, but relations became strained between the New York Indians and the Menominees who were actually residents on the Fox River land, resulting in the most complicated set of Indian land transactions in Wisconsin.

The Oneidas ended up with their present reservation in 1838 on part of the old 1823 tract. The Stockbridge-Munsees and Brothertowns accepted contiguous reservations on the east side of Lake Winnebago in 1831 but sold the eastern half of their lands in 1839. One group of Stockbridges used their money to resettle west of the Mississippi, but nearly all perished as a result of hardship and disease; a few survivors straggled back to Wisconsin. The Brothertowns, in order to avoid removal to Kansas, agreed to the division of their remaining land into individually owned parcels. In so doing, they were the first Indians to become United States citizens and, as far as the federal government was concerned, non-Indians, although the government never informed them by treaty or other official document that it had ceased to recognize them. Despite subsequent loss of their land through fraud and tax foreclosures and the need to disperse to find means of survival, they maintained their tribal ties and certainly don't consider themselves non-Indians.

The Stockbridge-Munsees were declared citizens by an Act of Congress in 1843, but with knowledge of the Brothertowns' experience they lobbied successfully for its repeal in 1846. They ceded the western half of their Lake Winnebago land in 1848 and held out against removal until they signed a treaty on February 5, 1856, accepting a reservation to be established south of the Menominee Reservation boundary. Less than a week later, however, a treaty with the Menominees carved two townships out of the southwest corner of the Menominee Reservation to create a reservation for some Stockbridge-Munsees. The land was of poor quality for farming, and some Stockbridges moved onto the Menominee Reservation to survive while others scattered; many Munsees tried, without success, to resettle in their New York homeland. In 1871 the two-township reservation was reduced to half a township by an Act of Congress, the culmination of fraud and deception on the part of government representatives in collusion with whites interested in timber on the Stockbridges' land.

The Winnebagos/Ho-Chunks represent a third distinctive linguistic stock, Siouan. They are the descendants of people who stubbornly refused to leave Wisconsin despite several federal efforts to remove them by force. They lived in hiding and if caught managed to get back to Wisconsin. When the general Homestead Act of 1862 was amended in 1875 (and further amended in 1881) to include special provisions for Indians, they secured their residence in Wisconsin as homesteaders. Although this arrangement is not unique to the Winnebagos, they happen to be the only tribe in Wisconsin that benefited from this nineteenth-century policy alternative to reservations. They were then recognized as separate from those Winnebagos who had agreed to removal and have a reservation in northeastern Nebraska. People from the two groups visit each other and intermarry, but because a person can be enrolled in only one recognized tribe, the children of such unions have to be enrolled in either Nebraska or Wisconsin.

Individually held tracts of Winnebago land are scattered over a dozen Wisconsin counties, and a few are found in Minnesota opposite the La Crosse, Wisconsin, area. In addition to dispersed households, there are settlements of a few hundred acres each of tribal land near Black River Falls (the largest area, and where the tribal headquarters is located), Wittenberg, Wisconsin Rapids, Wisconsin Dells, Tomah, and La Crosse. This development will be considered in more detail in chapter 6 in regard to the more recent aspects of Indian policy.

Old residents, the Winnebagos are believed by archeologists to be a thrust of Siouan speakers from the lower Mississippi Valley who entered Wisconsin long before white contact. Besides their distinctive language, the Winnebago culture at the time of contact in the seventeenth century differed from that of the surrounding Algonkian speakers in religious cosmology and complexity of social organization. They had a very large, permanent village on Green Bay and extensive gardens but hunted and foraged seasonally all the way to the Mississippi River. At about the time of European contact they suffered a series of catastrophes, including warfare with coalitions of Algonkian-speaking enemies and one or more devastating epidemics. Research since the 1960s has begun to reveal the tremendous impact of European diseases on the native peoples of the Americas, beginning with infections borne inland from one group to another ahead of any actual meeting with Europeans. While all the Wisconsin tribes felt the impact of new diseases, the vividness of the effects of disease in Winnebago oral tradition and its special mention in the earliest documents regarding the tribe suggest that they were particularly hard hit because of their concentration in large communities. The Winnebagos became increasingly Algonkianized, particularly in material culture, because in the course of building back population loss they found spouses among their former enemies and more easterly tribes that sought temporary refuge in Wisconsin during the mid-seventeenth century to escape Iroquois incursions. These Algonkian influences as well as the economic requirements of the fur trade encouraged Winnebago expansion and dispersal into smaller village units. They gradually withdrew from their first recorded location on

Green Bay to fill the lands bounded by the Fox-Wisconsin and Rock River systems as this territory was vacated by newcomers, such as the Sauk and Fox, and such old residents as the Kickapoos and Santee Sioux, all of whom moved farther west.

✖ 3 ✖
FEDERAL INDIAN POLICY—
THE FORMATIVE YEARS

A s noted, virtually every experiment in the history of Indian policy has been tried out on one tribe or another in Wisconsin, but it seems that no matter what the government attempted, the effect was progressive impoverishment of the Indian people. The question arises how all this came about.

American policy, including treaties and reservations, derives from British precedents. As a result of boundary disputes among the New England colonies regarding land that they or individual residents allegedly bought from the Indians, it was decided early that negotiations with Indians concerning land, trade, and other matters would be the responsibility of the crown through its designated representatives on what today would be termed a government-to-government basis. Similarly, Indian affairs became a federal rather than state responsibility under Article I, Section 8-B of the United States Constitution: "The Congress shall have the power . . . to regulate commerce with foreign nations, and among the several states, and with the Indian tribes."

At first the federal government was most concerned with trade and keeping peace with the Indians, but as settlers pressed into the Indians' territory, special treaty commissions negotiated the purchase of Indian land, with the tribes reserving small parcels as homelands under federal jurisdiction and protection. To deal with the mounting volume of Indian business, a special Indian Office was created within the Department of War in 1824. Gradually enlarged and renamed the Office of Indian Affairs and eventually the Bureau of Indian Affairs, it was trans-

ferred to the newly created Department of the Interior in 1849. Some
Indian people believe Indian affairs should be in the State Department,
befitting nations, and not in the Department of the Interior along with
parks.

Although the price paid for Indian land averaged only about ten
cents an acre, American law specified that tribes were to be paid for
their land. Contrary to the popular impression, the buying-off (with or
without prior hostilities), removal, and containment of Indians did not
proceed in an orderly fashion as the frontier moved westward. Indian
people resisted not only by force of arms but also by protracted bargaining and an ineffable talent for obfuscation and delay. Few tribes sold all
their land at once but rather, under pressure, relinquished it a parcel at a
time, endeavoring to hold out on reduced land bases in their old territories. The Indian Removal Act passed in 1830, early in the administration
of Andrew Jackson, made explicit what had long been implicit in federal
policy: move the Indians entirely out of the eastern United States and
resettle them on reservations across the Mississippi River. As a result
there are no reservations in states along the Ohio River, where Jackson's
policy was first implemented.

Although some treaties contain poetic imagery, even the matter-of-
fact wording of most treaties that established reservations leaves no
doubt that Indians signed them with the idea of reserving small parts of
the country to be held and used tax-free as homelands forever, without
any date or condition to eventually relinquish them. Obviously, the government made promises in order to get negotiations settled as expedi-
tiously as possible. It did not expect to be held to account in perpetuity
— or even for very long. Even whites who supported removal on hu-
manitarian grounds to isolate Indians from the hostile forces and cor-
rupting influences of the frontier did not expect them to survive
indefinitely *as Indians*, holding the government to its promises, but rather
assumed they would blend into oblivion as a result of learning to live like
whites and embracing Christian precepts.

The white treaty commissioners never came out and said what was
really in the back of their minds, so the Indian leaders signed treaties
(with "his X mark"), trusting the words as translated to them. The fact
was that in the nineteenth century Indian people were dying off faster
than they were reproducing and had become accustomed to a wide
array of goods of white origin. What the treaty makers did not antici-

pate was that by 1900 the Indian demographic decline would level off and that in the next decade the Indian population would begin making a comeback. The government and non-Indians in general were influenced in their thinking by gross population statistics, which included western tribes just beginning to experience significant white contact and major epidemics. Had the treaty makers glanced eastward at the Indians longest in contact with whites, they would have seen that not all of them had vanished and their population had ceased decreasing. Natural selection had weeded out those most prone to diseases introduced from Europe. Indian groups had assimilated individuals of European ancestry and remained Indians, just as Europeans assimilated individuals of Indian ancestry without losing their social identity. The admixture of European genes in the Indian population is believed to have conferred some resistance to European diseases on surviving Indians. Many tribes were wiped out on the eastern seaboard, but a surprising number remain. Some, like the Pamunkey of Virginia, reside on state-administered reservations, legacies of the colonial past. Others simply persist as Indian enclaves among white neighbors.

If promises contained in treaties and other legal agreements were made carelessly by the government, these promises still are a central issue for Indian people. In addition to basing policy on a superficial understanding of population statistics, the government and the white population in general expected the white way of life to prevail in phasing out Indian distinctiveness. Few whites noticed that Indians acquired new items by picking and choosing what they could rework to make peculiarly their own. Since time immemorial the tribes had depended on trade and travel for things they did not produce or find in their own territories; witness such examples as shells from the Gulf of Mexico in archeological sites in Wisconsin and artifacts made of Lake Superior copper in the Ohio Valley. They had formal procedures to establish intertribal contracts for purposes of trade and alliances. They dealt with Europeans as they would with representatives of different Indian groups, and the Europeans accepted that the tribes were sovereign entities.

The various tribes entered into treaties and compacts with a succession of European powers and sometimes played them off against each other. For the most part the Wisconsin tribes initially allied themselves with the French against the British and, after 1763 when the French acknowledged defeat in the French and Indian War, with the British against the Americans in the Revolutionary War and the War of 1812. The few tribes who had supported the Americans fared no better after the hostilities than those who had supported the British. The United States entered into treaties with the Indian tribes from the founding of the republic until 1871, but even after that date official "agreements" were made that resembled treaties in their wording and their promises to deal with loose ends left after the treaty period.

In Wisconsin, as had happened farther east and was to happen later in the West, the lands relinquished by one tribe were sometimes used and occupied for a considerable period as a regular homeland by another tribe that had been pushed on by the frontier ahead of white settlement. Thus, although the government had bought a large part of the land in southwestern Wisconsin and northwestern Illinois acquired in a treaty with the Sauk and Fox tribes in 1804, the government repurchased the same land in smaller parcels between 1816 and 1832 from the Winnebagos and Potawatomis who had established residence there. (An intriguing, unexplained feature of the Potawatomi Treaty of 1829 but not unique to it is that the careful reader will note "her X mark" after five of the thirty-five names.)

A dissident band of Sauks under the leadership of Black Hawk resented the 1804 sale and nourished the hope that the British would return and defeat the Americans. In 1832 Black Hawk led his band of about one thousand men (of whom some four hundred were armed and mounted warriors), women, and children back east across the Mississippi in an attempt to reestablish their old tribal settlement in northwestern Illinois. Although Black Hawk soon perceived the futility of the venture, he was unable to communicate his desire to surrender to the militia and regular troops pursuing him in order to secure the safe return of his band to Iowa. There are many accounts detailing the so-called war Black Hawk did not want but could not avoid; in short, he led a convoluted retreat of delaying actions against his pursuers up the Rock River in Illinois and then west through the rugged "driftless area" of southeastern Wisconsin. Exhausted, many died along the way before reaching the mouth of the Bad Axe River where it empties into the Mississippi. There they were cut off and decimated in a bloody slaughter while attempting to cross the river to the Iowa side. A small contingent had remained loyal to Black Hawk, who had left a day or two before the carnage to seek refuge among the Chippewas. They were intercepted by some Winnebagos who persuaded Black Hawk to accept their offer of safe conduct to Prairie du Chien, where he then made his formal surrender.

Despite Black Hawk's independent action, the tribal organization of the Sauks, like the Fox, Menominee, Potawatomi, and Winnebago tribes, included an overall sense of unity, concepts of tribal rather than just band chieftainship, and a tendency to expand into new territory or relinquish territory as a concern of the entire tribe. In comparison, the Ottawas and Chippewas were loose congeries of relatively autonomous bands united by knowledge of common ancestry and shared traditions and customs. Nevertheless, at some unknown date, they and the more tightly knit Potawatomis formed an alliance known as the "Three Fires." Thus, in 1829 and 1833 when the Potawatomis signed treaties ceding what clearly was their land, a few Ottawas and Chippewas living among them at the time also signed the treaties, but their signatures had no bearing on land occupied by Chippewa and Ottawa bands in northern Michigan and Wisconsin. In a similar situation in 1827, some Chippewas signed the treaty concerning the New York Indians along with the Menominees, who were the regular residents of the area. The Winnebagos also were signatory because their prior occupancy and long-standing friendship were still honored by the Menominees in negotiations concerning the land. This treaty also illustrates that things are not what they seem in black and white: the treaty lists the tribes alphabetically, which gives the Chippewas an appearance of primacy, and the Winnebago signers' names are not distinguished from those of the Menominees.

All the component bands or villages of the more tightly structured tribes felt a common concern in any treaty entered into, whether or not they were located in an area being ceded. Since it often was difficult to get consensus among the various communities of a tribe in regard to land sales, the white treaty makers often settled for what seemed to them a majority of signatures of important men of the tribe — or men they took it upon themselves to designate as chiefs. Dissatisfaction with treaty negotiations sometimes created dissident factions who, even among the closely knit tribes, withdrew their cooperation. When the treaty-abiding faction had moved on, the government often had difficulty dealing with the dissidents, who were obliged to look out for themselves. Eventually they might be treated as a separate entity as the government sometimes dealt with isolated bands of the loosely knit tribes. Consequently, the format of treaties gives the misleading impression that all of the tribes in a given region had the same structure.

Although the government began entering into treaties in the Wisconsin-Illinois region before the War of 1812 and immediately thereafter, primarily to win allies away from the British, it was the Treaty of 1825 at Prairie du Chien that heralded systematic negotiations for the Indians' lands and underlies the present situation. The government called a great intertribal council and asked the tribes to set forth their boundaries, ostensibly to assure peace among them but really as a preliminary to negotiate with them for their lands. Map 2 (page 7) shows land cessions and their dates, beginning in southern Wisconsin (also reaching into Illinois) with the Potawatomis and Winnebagos. By the 1820s lead miners were overrunning this area, inevitably resulting in hostile encounters. By 1827 the sorely aggravated Winnebagos sought revenge. A warrior named Red Bird and two companions were designated for the task. Although apparently not eager for the assignment, they finally attacked a settler's home and killed several people. When the government threatened wholesale reprisal unless the perpetrators were handed over, Red Bird and his accomplices surrendered voluntarily and were sentenced to be hanged. The Winnebagos were advised to seek a presidential pardon, but the price turned out to be the cession of tribal lands encompassing the lead mines. By the time the treaty was carried out in 1829, Red Bird had died in prison at Prairie du Chien.

Black Hawk had found allies among some of the Winnebagos who had remained in the area ceded along the Rock River in 1829, particularly White Cloud, known as the Winnebago Prophet, whose brother was with Black Hawk when he surrendered to the Winnebagos. Winneshiek, a prominent Winnebago chief, moved his village from the Rock River to Minnesota to avoid getting embroiled in the war, but one of his sons joined Black Hawk. The government then convinced the Winnebagos to sell the adjoining eastern portion of their land in 1832, claiming that it could not guarantee protection of the tribe from white settlers outraged by the recent hostilities. Since the Winnebagos' northern and least productive area could not support the whole tribe, many villagers from the ceded lands moved to an area set aside for them in northeastern Iowa as part of the payment for their 1832 cession.

The Treaty of 1837 ceded the last of the Winnebagos' homeland, a treaty the entire tribe considered invalid, even fraudulent. It was egregiously shabby treatment of the people who had facilitated Black Hawk's apprehension five years earlier. Despite pressure from the government, the tribe had repeatedly refused to even discuss selling this land but finally agreed to an invitation to send a delegation to Washington, D.C. on the understanding that they would just talk about why they had to keep this land. They purposely sent a group lacking the requisite representation of the Bear Clan with authority to sell land. Although they eventually signed in order to get home and hunt to support their families before winter set in, they warned the treaty commissioners not to expect their people to abide by the treaty. They had held out for a period of eight years before they had to leave Wisconsin, in an effort to buy time to renegotiate. The treaty actually reads "eight months." As discussed, the Winnebagos who had traditionally resided in the 1837 cession remained there and lived a fugitive existence until they were able to take up homesteads in Wisconsin.

Meanwhile, the Winnebagos who had settled on a reservation in Iowa after 1832 were caught in hostilities between the Sauks and the eastern Sioux and in 1846 finally were allowed to sell this land by treaty and move to a reservation in central Minnesota. This also proved unsatisfactory, as they were then caught in hostilities between the Chippewas and Santee Sioux. The treaty of 1855 granted them a smaller but agriculturally desirable reservation where their agent praised them for their sobriety and diligence. In 1859 they ceded the less productive western half of the reservation to pay for improvements on the eastern half. The Winnebagos took no part in the Sioux uprising that occurred in Minnesota during the Civil War. In fact, a number of young Winnebago men were away serving as volunteers in the Union Army. Yet the Winnebagos, peacefully settled in Minnesota, were rounded up along with the Sioux (not all of whom had participated in the uprising) and summarily moved by Executive Order of President Lincoln to a barren reservation on Crow Creek, South Dakota. Hastily fashioning dugouts, the Winnebagos fled down the Crow Creek to the Missouri River and eventually found sanctuary among the Omahas in northeastern Nebraska, where their reservation was established in 1865.

About a month before making the controversial Treaty of 1837 with the Winnebagos, the government negotiated successfully with the Santee Sioux for their land in Wisconsin. The Santees had already pretty

well decamped across the Mississippi, and the Winnebagos and Chippewas were hunting into their area. The Chippewas also gave up a large
tract in western Wisconsin in 1837 and their land along Lake Superior in
1842.

The Menominees ceded their land in nine parcels over a period of
twenty-one years beginning in 1827. Except for the Oneida Reservation
established in 1838, by 1848 all Indian land in Wisconsin had been sold
to the United States and all the Indians were supposed to be resettled
across the Mississippi. Then policy changed in 1848. Although the eastern tribes were considered "pacified" in the language of the day, they
were still disgruntled, and the long struggle to defeat the Plains tribes
was just getting under way. Resettling all the tribes in one great western
Indian territory posed the danger that they might set aside old differences and unite against the whites. Wisconsin tribes had been involved
in such alliances under Pontiac in the early 1760s and under Tecumseh
in the War of 1812.

The new policy was designed to settle tribes safely separated from
one another, even in parts of their old homelands if such land was not
attractive to whites. Thus, Wisconsin represented a kind of watershed in
the history of Indian policy, with the Oneidas, Stockbridge-Munsees,
and Brothertowns already moved here from a more easterly location,
earlier Wisconsin residents such as the Sauks, Foxes, Kickapoos, and
Santee Sioux moved farther West, and the Winnebagos and Potawatomis divided between western reservations and their Wisconsin
homelands.

The policy change was reinforced by growing white sympathy to let
the Indians stay because of a dreadful incident affecting the Chippewas
in the winter of 1850–1851. The government paid for the tribes' lands on
an installment system. Treaties specified the amount to be paid as annuities over a period of usually thirty or forty years, and the Indian people
depended on this money until they could be reestablished on permanent
reservations. The Chippewas' annuities were paid in the fall at La
Pointe, centrally located on Madeline Island, but since the Wisconsin
Chippewas were supposed to choose reservations in the Minnesota Territory, the Commissioner of Indian Affairs, Luke Lea, thought he could
lure them west by moving the payment to Sandy Lake on the upper Mississippi, some three to five hundred miles from the Wisconsin villages.
Lea was under pressure from the governor of the Minnesota Territory

and settlers there because local economies benefited wherever Indian annuity payments were made. Tradesmen inflated prices for supplies the Indians needed, and there were always opportunities for graft and kickbacks. The Chippewas arrived in October, becoming ever more destitute, as game was scarce. They waited six weeks for the person in charge of distributing payments, and then he arrived empty-handed. Congress had failed to appropriate funds in time to make the payments. With winter closing in, and unable to obtain supplies, it is estimated that more than three hundred Chippewas died of exposure and starvation trying to get back home.

The Menominee, Stockbridge-Munsee, and four of the Chippewa reservations were established by treaty under the new policy and, as already discussed, the government eventually got around to dealing in various ways with the Winnebagos and Potawatomis and the two overlooked bands of Chippewa.

WHi(X3)11633

Yellow Thunder, born in the late eighteenth century, was a leader of the "Disaffected Winnebagos," those Ho-Chunks who opposed the Treaty of 1837 ceding their last land in Wisconsin. Forcibly removed to Iowa in 1840 with other members of his tribe, he soon escaped back to Wisconsin and induced a white sympathizer to interpret his request to purchase forty acres at the government land office at Mineral Point. Since the clerks could find no law prohibiting such an action by an Indian, Yellow Thunder secured his residence in Wisconsin. He died in 1874, just before the right to take up homesteads was granted to all Winnebago refugees in Wisconsin.

IU

OTOSHKI-KIKINDIUIN

AU

TEBENIMINUNG GAIE BEMAJIINUNG

JESUS CHRIST:

IMA

OJIBUE INUEUINING GIIZHITONG.

THE

NEW TESTAMENT

OF

OUR LORD AND SAVIOUR JESUS CHRIST:

TRANSLATED INTO THE LANGUAGE

OF THE

OJIBWA INDIANS.

NEW YORK:

AMERICAN BIBLE SOCIETY,

INSTITUTED IN THE YEAR MDCCCXVI.

1875.

New Testament in Ojibwa Language, 1875, one of many translations of the Bible into Indian languages.

WHi(X3)12939

Federal agents paying annuities to Chippewa Indians at La Pointe, 1869.

WHi(X3)23295

Indian School, Sawyer County, circa 1885.

Mr. and Mrs. Joseph Monegar, Ho-Chunk, Black River Falls, circa 1909. Typical of Indian portraits of this period, women wore traditional finery while men often wore white clothing styles.

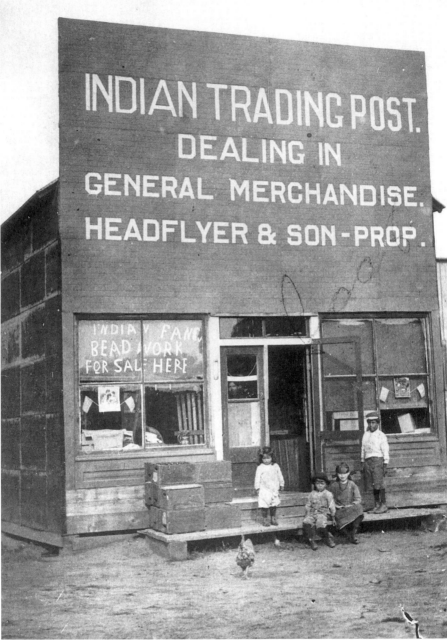

Trading post, Lac du Flambeau, circa 1910.

WHi(X3)12052

Oneida Reservation fair, 1899, demonstrating the commitment to agricultural pursuits just as the effects of the General Indian Allotment Act of 1897 were getting under way to deprive the Oneida of most of their land by 1934.

Prairie Band Potawatomi families who returned to Wisconsin from Kansas around 1900 bought land at Powers Bluff (also called Skunk Hill) in Wood County. A mixed tribal settlement developed that also included Ho-Chunk, Menominee, and Chippewa people. Records are not clear regarding how the Indians lost their

WHi(X3)35356

land, but in 1938 Wood County turned Powers Bluff into a public park. In 2000, when the county planned to expand its winter tubing and skiing trails, it was opposed by descendants of the old settlement because of family graves in the area. They were joined by environmentalists and archeologists concerned about the unusual plant life at Powers Bluff and ancient archeological sites there.

A largely Menominee logging crew, circa 1909.

WHi(X3)25448

United States Indian School baseball team, Lac du Flambeau, circa 1925.

WHi(X3)15499

Chippewa canoe maker, Lac du Flambeau, 1927.

Chippewa man harvesting wild rice on the Bad River Reservation, 1941. Bureau of Indian Affairs, Department of the Interior.

✿ 4 ✿

ADMINISTERING
INDIAN AFFAIRS

Until the close of the nineteenth century, when BIA personnel were included in the federal civil service, political patronage and outright corruption were part and parcel of the reservation system. Because regional superintendents and local Indian agents usually served only as long as their political party was in power in Washington, it was almost expected that they would line their own pockets at the Indians' expense. At annuity payment time, traders would set forth debts supposedly owed by individual Indians, and the agent would deduct these from the sum due the tribe at large before distributing the rest among the tribe members. The system lent itself to inflated debts and kickbacks, because the agent determined whether or not a trader had a legitimate claim. Kickbacks also occurred in the letting of contracts to suppliers of goods and services specified in treaties along with annuities.

When annuities ran out, most Indians simply could not support themselves on the reservations, and Congress made annual appropriations for basic subsistence — another source of graft. This is not to say there were no honest and idealistic people who saw the need for long-range programs for the Indian communities to pull themselves out of poverty, but they could accomplish little given the uncertainty of their terms of employment and a distant Congress more or less indifferent to the critical needs of people who were expected to vanish soon anyway. Rations and blankets were considered sufficient to "smooth the dying pillow."

In 1831 the unfortunate term *ward* entered the vocabulary of Indian affairs. John Marshall, Chief Justice of the Supreme Court, drew an analogy to the responsibility of a guardian to protect the property of a ward in his explanation of the federal government's constitutional responsibility to protect the Indians' tribally held lands from appropriation by states or individuals. The matters at issue concerned the Cherokees, but Marshall's interpretation of the Constitution was meant to apply to "the Indian tribes" in general. He also defined tribes as "domestic dependent nations," an admittedly unusual but genuine self-governing entity that had not relinquished sovereignty over its own lands when it put itself under the protection of "a stronger nation" by treaty. In the 1860s, the label *ward* was dusted off and given a new meaning to indicate that Indians as individuals were the responsibility of the Department of the Interior and not fair game for indiscriminate hostilities by the War Department.

As tribes were settled on reservations, however, BIA administrators on the reservations came to interpret their role — though it was never a matter of law — as literal "guardians" who could manage the personal lives of Indian "wards" and make decisions for them as if they were minor children who were both slow and recalcitrant to learn. As tribes struggled to get on their feet and make new social and economic adaptations as ongoing communities, the Bureau worked just as hard to de-Indianize, individualize, and remold them in the image of white farmers.

In 1871, the government decided not to make any more Indian treaties. Most Indian land had been acquired anyway, and most Indians were assigned reservations. Although existing treaties were officially still in effect, in practice the key to dealing with the tribes was to be vigorous repression of things Indian, by both law and day-to-day administration, so as to "break the tribal tie" by undercutting traditional patterns of leadership, law, social control, and religion. In the Annual Reports of the Commissioner of Indian Affairs, along with statistics from the various reservations on the numbers of acres plowed and bushels of crops raised, there are entries concerning the number of Indian men and women who regularly wore "citizen's clothing" and men who had cut their long hair.

Children were hauled off to distant boarding schools, first established in the late 1870s, where they wore military-style uniforms and their lives were regimented; boys learned manual skills, girls learned housekeeping, and both learned only the basics of reading, writing, and "ciphering." They were punished severely if caught speaking their own languages. Ironically, as students who spoke different tribal languages were forced to learn English, they could communicate with each other, and they gained a sense of Indianness and common problems transcending tribal differences. The early leadership of pan-Indian struggles for Indian rights sprang from the boarding schools. Eventually enough boarding schools were built so that children sometimes did not have to go far from home. The one at Tomah, for example, served Wisconsin tribes. Religious denominations also established boarding and day schools that were still operating well into the twentieth century.

Meanwhile, on the reservations Indian people chafed under disparagement and interdiction of their customary practices. Sincere reformers, concerned about the poverty and related social problems of apathy and drinking on the reservation, were convinced that the Indians would never "progress," despite the best efforts of the BIA and Christian missions to turn them into farmers, until they owned private property. It was not a new idea, as evidenced by Indian homesteads and the division of the Brothertowns' reservation. The solution to the "Indian problem" across the nation, however, was to be the Dawes Act, or General Indian Allotment Act, of 1887, which was enthusiastically passed over the few voices raised against it in Congress by people who knew the earlier experiments were turning out badly. The Act provided for the division of the reservations into 160-acre parcels for each family head, 80 acres for each single person over eighteen and for minor orphans, and 40 acres for single people under eighteen. Adjustments were permitted where the nature of the land suggested larger acreages. The allotments were to be tax free and could not be sold for twenty-five years, about a generation, by which time the reformers expected the Indians would have severed their tribal ties in favor of personal gain.

Individuals could choose their own land, but if they rejected the idea of allotment, the agent chose land for them. Land left over on the reservation after the Indians received their allotments was considered "surplus" that the government could open to public sale, the proceeds earmarked for the government to oversee the purchase of livestock, plows, and the like to help the Indians get established. The great Indian land grab began. It was soon apparent that the desired transition from tribal member to independent farmer might take more or less than twenty-five years, and later legislation required that an Indian be declared "competent" before receiving a "fee patent" to do as he wished with his land. Although "surplus" land was bought quite legally, land-hungry whites in connivance with unscrupulous Indian agents regularly abused the "competency" provision. People who could not read or write or even speak English were declared competent to sell their land only a few years after getting their allotments. Nationally, between 1887 and 1934, reservation land was reduced from some 150 million acres to about 50 million acres.

In Wisconsin, about half of the total reservation acreage was lost, in contrast to the almost three-quarters loss sustained across the country. This was primarily because the scheduled allotment of the Menominee Reservation, the largest in the state, was never carried out. The tribe had developed a sustained-yield system of lumbering that required an undivided land base to succeed. However, allotment nearly wiped out the Oneida Reservation by the 1930s, while the Stockbridge Reservation was eliminated through a variation on the usual allotment procedures. In 1910, all the land was divided and fee patents were issued, taking the reservation out of tribal trust status.

Like treaties, allotment was based on the premise that the Indian population would dwindle away, but those allottees who escaped the honor of "competency" passed their property on to increasing numbers of descendants after the end of the nineteenth century. The subdivision of land became even more complicated, because people inherit not only from parents but also from siblings and further-removed kin who have no direct descendants. It is not uncommon for an Indian person to have as much as twenty or thirty acres but in numerous, sometimes ridiculously small parcels all over the reservation. The BIA soon began to handle the growing "heirship" problem by renting out large tracts to whites for large single-crop or livestock enterprises and dividing the rent money among the many owners. By the end of the nineteenth century, even experienced white farmers were finding it increasingly difficult to support themselves on the kind of small, subsistence farms envisioned in the allotment policy and welcomed the availability of low-rent Indian land.

While the Oneida and Stockbridge Reservations were desirable farmland, the northerly location of the Chippewa reservations made them poor prospects for farming. Even the Chippewa Treaty of 1854 recognized that commercial fishing, which the Lake Superior groups had long engaged in, was their most feasible source of support. Lumbering and, later, resort development and wealthy urbanites' desire for summer homes attracted whites when Chippewa land became available through allotment. The Winnebago homesteads, generally only forty to sixty acres to begin with, became divided through inheritance like the reservation allotments and, until the practice was stopped in the 1930s, the land often was put on county tax rolls without the owners' knowledge and lost through tax default.

The renting out of allotted land gave rise to a widespread but erroneous idea that the government pays every Indian person a monthly stipend for no particular reason but federal benevolence. It is a source of a good deal of bitter "Don't I wish!" joking among Indian people. Allotment is the major cause of Indian grievance expressed in the phrase "Broken Treaties!" Non-Indians tend to misunderstand the words as a reference to the Indians being cheated out of the whole continent in treaty negotiations, a matter with which they can afford to be sympathetic but cannot change and thus feel no responsibility. The summer home or resort they enjoy "Up North," however, might well be on old allotted Indian land. When treaties were made, the Indians knew they were bargaining at a disadvantage but, outnumbered and outarmed, they held out for small tribal homelands to develop their own means of survival under changed circumstances. The Indians assumed that if either side contemplated other arrangements, they would work it out on a government-to-government basis. The United States decided unilaterally and over Indian protest to allot the reservations that supposedly were guaranteed to the Indians. The tribes had signed treaties trusting in this promise. The American nation was guilty of both bad faith (another Indian rallying cry) and bad judgment, because allotment was a disaster from which the tribes are still trying to recover.

❦ 5 ❦

TWO WORLD WARS AND
THEIR AFTERMATHS

When the United States entered the First World War in 1917, many Indians were not citizens and therefore could not be drafted. Nevertheless, they volunteered in large numbers and compiled a remarkable record of heroism. Newspapers reported their deeds and the fact of dreadful conditions on the reservations they came from. An aroused public prompted Congress in 1924 to grant citizenship to the Indians with particular stress on the right to vote. Some Indians already were enfranchised through certain features of allotment, some treaties, and special legislation, but for the most part they were not interested in voting. In fact, a great many Indian people were upset and angered by the Indian Citizenship Act, which appeared to them as simply another effort to diminish their tribal sovereignty and treaty rights.

A more meaningful result of wartime publicity was a major investigation of Indian problems undertaken at federal expense but conducted by a private research institute. The ten-person survey staff, directed by Lewis Meriam, included one Indian, Henry Rowe Cloud, a Nebraska Winnebago. Published in 1928, the Meriam Report, as it is commonly called, was ruthlessly thorough and reached some surprising conclusions and recommendations. It pointed out that as bad as conditions were, the only reason they were not worse was that the Indian people had somehow nurtured a semblance of community cohesion and traditional sharing that gave direction to life and enabled them to survive. Allotment, resulting in the continuing loss of land, was singled out as the primary cause of Indian despair, demoralization, and poverty. The unallotted Menominee tribe of Wisconsin was cited as one of the very few tribes that, while far from wealthy, was a great deal better off than the vast majority of tribes in the whole country. The tribally owned reservation, with its carefully managed forest and lumber mill, provided regular employment and supported community facilities and services.

Although still imbued with the idea that assimilation was both inevitable and desirable, the Meriam Report was harshly critical of BIA policies to stamp out Indian customs before adequate substitutes had been established and added the radical observation that everything Indian was not bad. The Report made a number of important recommendations, but before any action could be initiated the nation was overtaken by the Great Depression.

The election of Franklin D. Roosevelt brought a "New Deal" to Indian Affairs with the appointment of John Collier, Sr., to head the BIA. Collier and his staff actually went out and met with Indians to get their opinions on future policy. The Indian Reorganization Act (IRA) of 1934 was the major result of the Meriam Report, combined with Collier's own extensive familiarity with Indian problems. The IRA gave tribes the option (but did not require them) to organize, with their own constitutions and charters. They could enter into contracts with various federal agencies and the private sector and borrow from a revolving loan fund to forward their own social and economic plans. The original draft of the IRA would have granted broad authority to those tribes that wished to take over the operation of functions and services from the BIA along with direct access to funds and acquisition of Bureau buildings and equipment. Congress struck this enlightened provision from the Act. A critical weakness of the IRA that Congress added over Collier's opposition was that reservation superintendents held final veto power over the tribal governments' decisions to save the tribes from their own mistakes and also the opportunity to learn from them. Collier, furthermore, had to work with an inherited bureaucracy still strongly committed to the ancient objectives of de-Indianization and assimilation. Collier threatened the very nature of their universe. They sometimes came down with a heavy hand and lacked patience with Indian decision-making methods entailing long discussions eventually leading to consensus. Since the new tribal officers could only manipulate but not control power, Indian political life exhibited a tendency to elect people who were recognized as talented in dealing with the white bureaucracy but who also were suspected of sharing white values and tempted to use their offices for personal gain. Indian people have an abiding distaste for leaders who see themselves as bosses rather than spokespersons and advocates for community consensus.

Collier was criticized both for trying to impose white bureaucratic structures that would stifle the expression of traditional Indian concepts and for trying to turn back the clock to restore Indian customs that would undo the progress Indians had made away from traditional concepts.

Whatever the shortcomings of the IRA and its implementation, Collier's own good faith and understanding of Indian grievances were clear to the majority of tribes when he took immediate steps to halt the process of land loss set in motion by allotment and began efforts to restore tribal land. Although inadequately funded, the land acquisition program played a significant role in Wisconsin with the creation of the St. Croix and Mole Lake Reservations and the restoration of several thousand acres to the Stockbridge and Oneida tribes. The Stockbridges posed a special case because with no land in tribal trust status they were technically without a reservation and therefore ineligible to organize under the IRA. In 1937 they gained about one thousand acres of tribal trust land under the Collier administration, which allowed them to organize. By 1972 the tribe had regained about fifteen thousand acres of the original reservation as tribal trust land, much of it land that had passed to the Department of Agriculture as "surplus" land they had been allowed to use since 1948.

One of the many regional meetings to explain the IRA was held at Hayward, Wisconsin, in June of 1934. All of the Wisconsin tribes except the Winnebagos and the Menominees soon opted to organize. The Menominees declined because they already had an elected tribal government that had evolved as their lumbering enterprise required tribal approval of contracts. They did avail themselves, however, of certain provisions of the IRA giving them greater access to information about the management of their business affairs. The Winnebagos simply took no action for or against the IRA, fearing it might jeopardize their long-standing hope of collecting money they believed was owed to them from old treaty negotiations. Without a reservation they got very little help from the BIA but also were spared its excessive meddling in their affairs.

Apart from some housing built for them on federal land (but not Indian trust land) by the Work Projects Administration in the 1930s, they were generally neglected by the government and supported themselves by itinerant crop harvesting, other seasonal wage work, trapping, basketry, beadwork, and some gardening. The reservation Winnebagos in Nebraska readily accepted the IRA.

In further regard to the land issue, the Meriam Report staff noted that throughout the country they heard many grievances over unsettled land claims and recommended that these be handled by more expeditious and less expensive means than the cumbersome, costly, and usually disappointing process that required a jurisdictional act from Congress for each tribe to bring suit in the Court of Claims. In 1946 Congress finally passed the Indian Claims Commission Act, which allowed tribes to bring suit without cost and restricted attorneys' cuts of any awards to 10 percent. Claims had to be filed by 1951. Three presidentially appointed commissioners were expected to hear and settle all the claims by 1957, but the volume of claims — more than six hundred dockets — and the time-consuming procedures the Commission adopted eventually required doubling the number of commissioners and several extensions of its tenure, until it was terminated in 1978. The few remaining claims (mostly appeals) were transferred to the U.S. Court of Claims.

Although the Indian Claims Commission Act contains the broadest grounds for suit in the history of federal legislation, the Commissioners construed them as narrowly as possible, dismissing grievances over the effects of allotment at the outset as outside their jurisdiction. They could hear collective claims from "tribes, bands, and statutory groups," whereas, they ruled, allotments of tribal land were only an aggregate of individual grievances. It was the forced individualization of land that so many tribes were most aggrieved about, and the Commission used it against them when they tried to seek justice!

In some ways the Indian Claims Commission (ICC) reflected the last sentiments of the Collier administration in the sensitive wording of the Act passed in 1946, while its subsequent interpretation and implementation reflected the government's repudiation of Collier's philosophy at the end of the Second World War. The claims took decades to settle and were of negligible monetary importance — a thousand dollars or so per capita. And, once a distribution was accepted, there could never be an appeal or new litigation concerning the issues covered in the case. Yet the creation of the Commission itself has had profound and positive indirect effects. Prior to 1946, very few attorneys knew much about the law in relation to Indians, and few tribes understood the nature and potential importance of the courts to seek redress of grievances. With so many tribes and attorneys involved in the ICC, and because the claims mainly concerned inadequate payment for lands lost during the treaty period, a wealth of anthropological and historical documentation in the National Archives and other depositories was assembled and made accessible. Now Indian people can draw upon this source material as well as a knowledgeable cadre of both Indian and non-Indian lawyers and scholars.

Anthropology has attracted Indian people to its professional ranks since its inception in the nineteenth century and continues to do so, but since the 1960s the legal profession has held a special appeal for young Indian people. During the 1970s two organizations, the Native American Rights Fund and the Institute for the Development of Indian Law, were founded; they are staffed largely by Indian people to do legal work on behalf of Indian clients. Growing recourse to the law has related not only to settling old grievances but to warding off new threats to Indian rights that began about 1948 and forwarding new developments in Indian Country.

The Indian "New Deal" lasted only some seven years, from 1934 until the United States entered the Second World War in 1941. Funding for many federal agencies was redirected to the war effort, but more was involved in BIA cutbacks than wartime economics. Congress turned an increasingly deaf ear to Collier's pleas in the 1940s to keep new Indian programs alive and prepare for the problems the tribes would face in peacetime. With so many Indian people employed in defense industries and the armed services (more often than not they volunteered, including a high proportion of young women joining the new women's military units) and sending money back to the reservations, Indian poverty was temporarily alleviated. Indeed, Congress considered the problem permanently solved with the wartime exodus from the reservations. But Collier foresaw that when the war ended the Indian people would come home. The Indian population also shared in the postwar baby boom, and the already limited and undeveloped reservation resources were less adequate than ever to support decent community life. The war, nevertheless, had been a mass educational experience. People returned with new knowledge and skills, eager to make more informed use of the IRA through their tribal governments.

Seeing that the Indians were worse off than ever and that a large amount of money would be needed to get the clamoring Indian communities back on their feet and make up for ground lost during the war, Congress blamed Collier for the crisis he had merely predicted. Postwar problems were attributed to Collier's departure from the time-honored assimilationist policy. Borrowing the rhetoric of the black movement for civil rights while remaining slow and insensitive to addressing the needs of black people, the cry in Congress now was to "desegregate" and "integrate" the Indians, "free" them, make them "first class citizens."

Such words of hope for black people in the 1950s conveyed a chilling threat to Indian people, who recognized the Congressional slogan that really applied to them: "Get the government out of the Indian business." The reservations were not urban ghettos that had been allowed to deteriorate by indifferent slumlords; the reservations were the Indians' property. On most reservations allotment had resulted in a checkered pattern of Indian and white holdings — hardly a picture of segregation. No one tried to deny Indians the vote — quite the contrary! Racism is not unknown to Indian people, but ordinary white Americans will readily own up to and even boast about Indian forebears. Politicians and public figures capitalize on their Indian ancestry; even Winston Churchill claimed an Iroquois connection through his American mother's side of the family. Since the founding of the United States, Indian people had always been encouraged to disavow their cultural ties and become non-Indians by taking their names off tribal rolls.

Collier had understood — his detractors said he romanticized — the durability of Indian values and the persistence and growth of Indian communities despite ongoing assimilation of some individuals into the dominant society. He aspired to improve the Indians' collective lot by education and properly funded opportunities to experiment with community self-determination. Even those who might choose to leave would be better prepared to enter the white world at a decent socioeconomic level. But it would take time and money to enable the tribes, the poorest and most deprived of all Americans, to begin solving their own problems; Congress wanted a cheap, instant solution. Unable to prevail against Congress, Collier resigned in 1945. Few in the series of Collier's short-term successors tried to moderate between Congress and Indian interests as Collier saw them. The trend in the BIA was clearly directed toward a policy of terminating federal responsibility to protect the tribes' rights and lands. With Dwight D. Eisenhower's appointment of Glen Emmons as Commissioner of Indian Affairs in 1953, there was a complete takeover of the BIA, supported by Congress, by the forces that had opposed Collier.

❦ 6 ❦

TERMINATION
AND RELOCATION

During the treaty period and on up to Collier's administration, policy had been based on the expectation that the Indians would obligingly vanish. When they didn't, the policy of the 1950s was based on a two-pronged attack to make them go away. One prong was *termination*, set forth in House Concurrent Resolution 108 of 1953. The goal was to put an end to reservations, close off the tribal rolls, disregard federal pledges to protect Indian property and rights, and do it "with all possible speed." The other prong was *relocation*, a program to move the Indian people from their rural communities and disperse them in urban areas. Like all simplistic plans, the new policy was bound not only to fail but to create new problems. Intense Indian opposition to HCR 108 resulted in the grudging Congressional qualification that no tribe could be terminated without its prior agreement.

Legislation during the 1950s to reinforce the termination/relocation policy included Public Law 280, intended to make law enforcement on the reservations a state rather than a federal responsibility; however, with neither the states nor Indian people wild about the idea, PL 280 affected only five states, Wisconsin among them. Congress repealed the old Indian liquor law with a show of piety about correcting a case of racial discrimination, but some tribal councils were so appalled at the direction the government was taking that they promptly voted to keep their reservations dry. A further attempt to deny or erase Indian distinctiveness was the transfer of Indian Bureau health services to the general Public Health Service, which then found it necessary to establish a special Indian division to deal with the exceptionally severe health problems it had inherited.

In the 1950s, Wisconsin once again became a primary laboratory to tinker with new experiments in Indian policy. The moving force behind termination was a Republican senator from Utah, Arthur V. Watkins, who sought political immortality as the Indians' Lincoln, proclaiming, "These people shall be free!" The Menominee tribe, singled out in the Meriam Report, became Watkins's first target as most likely to succeed; he expected other tribes would then fall in line. The Menominees appeared exceptionally solvent. Thanks to access to their business records under the IRA, they instituted a suit against the federal government for mismanagement of their timber operation that dragged on for seventeen years but netted them an award of more than $7 million in 1951. With interest-bearing funds from the profits of their mill and forests, they had about $10 million in cash assets. The tribe had voted to use more than half of their award in per capita payments as compensation for money that individuals had not received through the years of mismanagement. The rest they earmarked for improvements to their hospital and other tribal purposes. Although it was the tribe's own money, Congress had to approve such expenditures; it released the improvement funds but held back on the per capitas.

Watkins ignored the reality that the Menominees were prosperous only in comparison to other tribes; their situation was, at best, precarious in relation to the nation as a whole. Increasing population since 1928 was straining their single-industry economy, and they hoped to use some of their award to explore new opportunities. The senator made a personal visit to the reservation in June of 1953, threatening the tribe that if they did not agree to termination voluntarily, Congress would terminate them anyway — and then, he implied, they would have no say in its terms. At his insistence the Menominee took a highly irregular vote, with a single "yes" or "no" approving *both* the release of their per capita payments (which they had already gone on record saying they wanted) and what Watkins termed "the principle of termination." Only five "no" votes were cast by a bare quorum of 174 people. Many had voted their opinion of termination with their feet by simply staying away from the discussion altogether. Two weeks later, after the issue was fully discussed and more clearly understood, another tribal council was convened, and the nearly 200 people present voted "no" unanimously to termination *even if it meant losing their per capitas.* Congress chose to ignore this forceful statement of community sentiment and a steady stream of subsequent petitions with many more signatures opposing termination. In June of 1954, the Menominee Termination Act was passed. The Menominees played for time, but after several delays the Act finally went into effect in 1961. It was an unmitigated disaster. (The effects of termination and the Menominee struggle for restoration are detailed in chapter 7.)

In the early 1950s, while Congress was pushing termination to pull the reservations out from under the tribes, the BIA instituted and hyped the euphemistically named Voluntary Relocation Program, which provided travel money to designated relocation cities around the country, preferably as far as possible from participants' reservations to discourage their returning home. Relocatees were helped to find their first housing and jobs, or job training, and then were expected to go it alone. People who had already taken up city life on their own terms did not need the program. The relocatees often were poorly screened in regard to their marketable skills, command of English, and urban experience. The mild recession of the 1950s left many families destitute, unable to get back to the reservations and shy or uninformed about seeking public assistance. Indeed, residency requirements in some cities made these new arrivals ineligible for welfare. They had traded reservation poverty for urban poverty that proved even worse. Their main help came from intertribal social organizations established by Indian people who, much earlier, had taken up city residence within reasonable "commuting" distance from their reservations. New Indian centers also developed to meet the crisis, supported by churches and other private sources of funding. Chicago, a designated relocation city for Indians far from the Midwest, had an established Indian population including many people from the Wisconsin tribes who were active in the Indian Center there and worked to assist the newcomers. The Bureau eventually set up relocation offices, mainly as information clearinghouses, in other cities such as Milwaukee where work was likely to be available to relocatees.

By the 1960 presidential campaign, both major parties recognized that Indian affairs were in a terrible mess. Indian people were eager to make their needs and wishes known and responded enthusiastically to the offer made in cooperation between the National Congress of American Indians (NCAI) and Sol Tax, an anthropology professor at the

University of Chicago. Informed and concerned Indian people had founded NCAI in 1945 to assist tribes in making effective use of the IRA when people would be back on the reservations after the war. By 1960, however, NCAI was occupied almost entirely in working and lobbying against the policy of the 1950s. Professor Tax offered to raise the money, handle logistics, and arrange for facilities if Indian people wanted to get together to see if they could agree among themselves on basic policy recommendations. His only condition was that any Indian person or group could attend and participate. NCAI provided the nucleus of an all-Indian Steering Committee to draw up a statement to start discussion. In June 1961, the largest and most representative gathering of Indian people to that date met for a week on the University of Chicago campus. The American Indian Chicago Conference (AICC) had been preceded by tribal and regional gatherings since the previous January, and the expanding Steering Committee met several times to sum up results and prepare representative samplings of individual letters to send to an ever-growing mailing list. Consensus had gradually evolved, culminating in the document completed at Chicago: *The Declaration of Indian Purpose*. An Indian delegation later presented the document to President John F. Kennedy in a ceremony on the White House lawn.

The AICC document emphatically opposed the policy of the 1950s, upheld tribal sovereignty and treaty rights as interpreted by John Marshall, and took up the cause of underserved and unrecognized tribes, but it reflected the moderate outlook that tribes should work within the existing system of federal administration. A small group at the Chicago gathering, including one member of the Steering Committee, argued for total independence of the reservations as sovereign nations in treaty relationships with the United States and Canada. To the moderates, this position was unrealistic and seemed to be inviting termination and loss of federal protection of Indian land. These "radicals" also supported the idea of picketing and public demonstrations, which the majority of people at Chicago frowned on as "not the Indian way" and likely to further confuse black and Indian issues in the public mind. When their position was rejected at the 1961 conference, the militant minority abstained from the final vote approving *The Declaration* and stalked out of the conference. Nevertheless, they had gained a wider hearing of their views through the AICC and made more of an impact than was initially realized.

Early in 1961 President Kennedy had appointed a task force to meet with Indian people around the country and prepare a report as a guide to future policy. The report paralleled the essential points of the AICC *Declaration*: insistence on the right to be Indian; protection of the Indian land base; education to advance tribal and individual goals; and community development programs, which also would be congruent with Indian values and cultural preferences. Philleo Nash, an anthropologist and former lieutenant governor of Wisconsin, was a member of the task force. In 1962 he was appointed Commissioner of Indian Affairs. Moving cautiously at first in the face of continuing assimilationist sentiment in Congress, Nash nevertheless inspired hope as "a new Collier." He stressed community development and humanized the relocation program to make it truly voluntary. Nash understood that while Indian people were interested in economic development, they needed to explore opportunities, discuss and weigh alternatives, and gain experience and confidence. Nash's superiors in the Interior Department and other interests who saw reservation development in terms of cheap labor pools for white capital deemed Nash's progress too slow. Nash saw no alternative but to resign. His tenure lasted just half as long as Collier's. He was succeeded by Robert Bennett, a Wisconsin Oneida, the first Indian to hold the office since Ely Parker during President Grant's administration. In the course of successive administrations, both Republican and Democrat, it became a matter of protocol that the head of the Indian Bureau must be an Indian.

Nash's brief term of office was to have great importance in Wisconsin. At the 1962 Midwest regional meeting of AICC held in Milwaukee, the group asked that Helen Miner Miller, a Wisconsin Winnebago and high school teacher, serve on the national Steering Committee. Inspired by this experience with the inner workings of AICC, Miller and other concerned and knowledgeable Winnebagos constituted themselves as the Wisconsin Winnebago Acting Business Committee. They applied successfully for a research grant from the Department of Health, Education, and Welfare entirely on their own initiative — a first in Indian affairs — to fund a detailed survey of all the scattered households. It was conducted by a bilingual team as a basis for future socioeconomic planning. Seeing the benefits of formal organization, and with the tribe's ICC claim under way, the Committee got tribal approval to apply for organization under the IRA. At first their efforts were blocked by the technical-ity that they had no reservation. Commissioner Nash assigned a deputy commissioner to the case, who discovered that many years earlier an old Winnebago homestead had automatically reverted to tribal trust status when the owner died without known heirs. This forty-acre "reservation" not only allowed the Wisconsin Winnebagos to become the first tribe to organize under the IRA since Collier retired, but also enabled them to acquire more land to qualify for housing projects, a high priority in the survey. Thus, in 1962, a year after termination became final for the Menominees, the Wisconsin Winnebagos launched a project that allows them to continue enlarging their acreage under tribal trust title. At present they have more than six thousand acres.

Organizations such as the NCAI and the dramatic model for intertribal cooperation afforded by the AICC influenced tribes around the country to form regional groupings for mutual help and political strength. In Wisconsin, the state's tribal governing bodies created the Great Lakes Intertribal Council (GLITC) in 1961. While still in its formative stage, GLITC responded to the request of the recently established Office of Economic Opportunity (OEO) to act as the central agency for the Wisconsin Indians. While OEO, as part of President Lyndon Johnson's "War on Poverty," was committed to grass-roots development, old bureaucratic tendencies were hard to overcome even in a new and innovative agency. The Winnebagos were actually set back for a time in the real grass-roots efforts they had made. Generally, however, OEO gave GLITC and its member tribes useful if sometimes painful experience in dealing with federal agencies besides the BIA and learning to tap nongovernmental sources of funding. Wisconsin Indians also benefited from another new federal agency. Wisconsin Judicare, first headed by Joseph Preloznik, was set up to assist any indigent people in the state's northern counties, which also happened to contain virtually all of Wisconsin's tribal communities.

As the threat of termination faded in the mid-1960s, the relocation program of the previous decade continued to have far-reaching consequences. In much the same way that boarding schools had inadvertently stimulated early pan-Indian sentiments and activism, relocation stimulated cooperation in the cities among people from many tribes.

Young Indian people born and reared in the cities tended to be imbued with their parents' heightened sense of Indianness as expressed through participation in intertribal organizations and the growing frequency of urban powwows. But they also were embittered by having been denied the opportunity to learn much about the life, traditions, and languages of their own tribes. Living for the most part in poor to actual slum neighborhoods, they brought streetwise assertiveness to their Indian grievances. They did not share the older generation's fear of demonstrations. They understood confrontation as a means of capturing public attention.

Although the first well-publicized Indian demonstrations, the fish-ins in the state of Washington in the 1960s, concerned treaty rights, it was the occupation of Alcatraz Island early in 1970 by San Francisco area relocatees and other Indian sympathizers that served dramatic and widely reported notice that "city Indians" could not be written off as lost in the urban crowd and that for Indian people the basic issues were still territory and treaties. The occupiers, calling themselves Indians of All Tribes, claimed Alcatraz on the basis of a Sioux treaty stating that abandoned federal property on the reservation would revert to the Indians. The claim had no substance in California, but the Indians capitalized on its symbolic meaning and planned to establish an intertribal community and cultural center at the former federal prison. They finally were forced to leave under a court order, but the occupation had a terrific inspirational impact on Indian people generally.

Meanwhile, closer to home, Indians in the Twin Cities formed the American Indian Movement (AIM) in 1968 initially to deal with problems they were having with law enforcement agencies. AIM chapters sprang up elsewhere, and AIM members could be counted on to converge from all over in support of local urban and reservation concerns. Although demonstrations were intended as a first step to evoke public interest in Indian problems, for many participants the demonstrations were therapeutic in themselves. Sometimes the follow-up was left to the dedicated handful of local people who could not always secure the beachheads.

It was during the relocation period that the term *Indian Country* seems to have acquired its present meaning and currency. Originally it meant only federal Indian trust land, but now it means any place where there is an active Indian presence, even the Internet.

❧ 7 ❧

MENOMINEE TERMINATION
AND RESTORATION

Although not wealthy, the Menominees in 1954 were paying their own way — even the salaries of BIA personnel. They supported the Catholic hospital and schools on the reservation and their own utility companies. They had chosen to operate their lumber industry to provide employment to anyone willing to work. For all that, they managed to make annual payments to tribe members and put aside savings to accrue interest. But by the time termination was in effect in 1961, the Bureau had let the already obsolete mill deteriorate further and done little to prepare the tribe to take over its management. Most of the tribe's working capital had been wiped out because the government had forced them to pay part of the cost of developing a termination plan they had not wanted in the first place. The Menominees had to sell the utility companies and close the hospital in which they had invested judgment money, and the new Menominee County had to contract for services with Shawano County. The termination plan created Menominee Enterprises, Inc. (MEI), which held all the former reservation land and assets and whose management was dominated philosophically by white businessmen serving with Menominee members. The Menominee people now owned stocks and bonds in a corporation that, unlike other such businesses, had a voting trust that actually held all the shares and voted those of minors and "incompetents" as a bloc.

The supposedly solvent and now "free" Menominees began termination with a $300,000 deficit and less control over and knowledge about their own affairs than they had under the most repressive and paternalistic BIA administrations. As the grim facts of the Menominee case became known (and the above doesn't begin to list all of them), it served to slow and finally end the termination policy, so only a few other tribes were terminated, notably the Klamath in Oregon and some small western groups. Furthermore, the once independent Menominees were costing the government money, as they needed infusions of emergency funding, for example, to deal with a tuberculosis epidemic and other health problems after the loss of their hospital.

Menominees' complaints about the management of MEI were dampened with the reminder that Menominee County was operating on a ten-year trial basis after termination took effect in 1961, and the state could choose to dismember it among neighboring counties in 1971, destroying any hope of maintaining the tribal estate and a semblance of home rule. Diffuse expressions of discontent finally crescendoed into angry, organized protest when MEI entered into a contract with a land developer to create artificial lakes and sell vacation homesites to non-Menominees. It was only the latest and most outrageous of a series of desperate measures to raise capital and lighten the county tax burden borne entirely by MEI. During 1970 a group of Menominees formed Determination of Rights and Unity for Menominee Shareholders (DRUMS), with chapters in Milwaukee and Chicago. Well educated, urban-based Menominees, such as the eloquent James White (Washinawatok) of Chicago, rallied the thoroughly intimidated people on the former reservation in a concerted effort to get termination repealed. Even the Menominees within MEI had always agreed that termination had been a mistake, but they considered its repeal an unrealistic dream and feared that agitation would destroy both the financially troubled corporation and the county.

DRUMS felt that the corporation and county were doomed anyway, and if they could not repeal termination, they would at least go down fighting. They prepared informational statements to hand out as they picketed at restaurants where promotional dinners were being provided for prospective buyers of vacation home sites. They also marched with signs at the Milwaukee office of the First Wisconsin Trust Company, which voted the shares of minors and incompetents and controlled MEI elections. They demonstrated at the land sales office at Keshena and along the main roads through Menominee County, bringing about the arrest of two DRUMS officers, Laurel Otradovic and Lloyd Powless, who accepted their stint in the Shawano County jail as prisoners of conscience. DRUMS protested at the land development company's headquarters in Reedsburg, a detour in an impressively coordinated week-long march from Keshena to Madison by several hundred Menominees and other Indian and non-Indian sympathizers in a successful bid to get Governor Patrick Lucey's support of the repeal of termination.

With legal counsel from Wisconsin Judicare, DRUMS harried MEI with litigation on various matters and mounted a proxy fight. Failing to garner enough votes to reorganize MEI — an option for 1971 built into the termination plan — because they did not control the minors' shares, DRUMS did manage to put its candidates in control of MEI and could begin to work toward its next objectives: phase out the land sales contract and repeal termination. Ada Deer, with a graduate degree in social work and experience in working in the BIA during the Nash era, moved to Washington, D.C., to direct the lobbying effort.

By this time Congress had formally abandoned the termination policy, but no one except the people associated with DRUMS believed it would ever change a decision on a tribe it had already terminated. And Congress did prove hard to persuade, but by the end of 1973 the Menominee Restoration Act was passed and signed into law by President Richard M. Nixon. The Act provided for the election of a Restoration Committee to undertake the complicated work of closing out contracts encumbering the tribal assets since termination, reorganizing the corporation, opening and updating the tribal roll, and creating a tribal government.

NARF augmented legal assistance from Judicare in the fight to repeal termination and convey the reservation back to federal status. The objective of the Restoration Committee, headed by Deer, "federal protection without federal domination," was not easily accomplished. The BIA was resistant to innovations in a tribal constitution that limited its role to protecting the land and tribal rights without meddling in the tribe's other affairs. On the other hand, a decade of termination had left a complicated legacy of financial and social problems that could not be overcome by the mere repeal of termination but required special skills, legal procedures, and time. In the last stages of the struggle for restoration, when most of the action had shifted from Wisconsin to Washington, D.C., it involved the active participation of only a few people. To many Menominees who missed the camaraderie, excitement, and sense of personal worth in doing something vital in the tribal interest, the

Restoration Committee appeared to be operating too much on its own initiative — much like the old MEI administration.

On New Year's Eve, 1974, a group calling itself the Menominee Warrior Society forcibly occupied a vacant novitiate facility belonging to the Roman Catholic Alexian Brothers and located just outside the reservation near the town of Gresham in Shawano County. The group claimed the property for the Menominee tribe to use as a hospital. The Warriors seemed to draw inspiration from the dramatic occupation of Alcatraz, the Indian takeover of the BIA building in Washington, D.C., and the protest at Wounded Knee, rather than from the more localized, sustained, and varied strategies undertaken by DRUMS, in which they had not been involved. Their perception appears to have been that direct action alone had toppled the old MEI and that it could topple the new tribal "establishment" to bring immediate benefits to the tribe. The Warriors attracted an interesting mix of supporters, from disaffected DRUMS people to old-guard MEI officers. The group also included some AIM observers and liberal-to-radical whites, most of whom had not been involved with DRUMS and really didn't understand what the occupation was all about but had become aware of the Menominees because of publicity DRUMS had gained for the tribe.

Initially the governor's representatives virtually ignored the Restoration Committee, the tribe's only elected officers, and tried to resolve the problem by negotiating solely between the Warriors and the Alexians. The Restoration Committee had immediately repudiated the Warriors' action as illegal, involving non-Menominee property, and laying claim to a white elephant that the Committee, as a provisional government, could not accept even if the Alexians offered it to the tribe. The Restoration Committee was dead right but came across as high handed, giving its detractors fuel for their accusations that the Committee members were insensitive to the grass roots people. The governor called in the Wisconsin National Guard almost immediately to forestall violence, and the Warriors withdrew after about a month in the novitiate, leaving it in a shambles. The Alexians later disposed of the property with no reference to the Menominees.

The reservation was shaken by further internal disturbances in the years following restoration, including several violent deaths. It took the Menominees five years to reach agreement on a constitution and the election of permanent officers. Meanwhile, the Restoration Committee obtained substantial federal grants and other funding to build a new health facility, get the mill into increasingly productive operation, and develop various programs to improve reservation conditions. As the Menominees restore themselves economically and socially, there also has been a revival of traditional religious practices that were just about moribund during termination.

Milwaukee Journal photo by Ernest W. Anheuser; WHi(X3)35360

Menominee efforts to restore the tribe's reservation and federal Indian status included the demonstration in 1971 in Milwaukee led by James White (Washinawatok), president of DRUMS, at the first Wisconsin Trust Company that, under termination, controlled a majority of the tribe's votes.

Milwaukee County Historical Society

Vacant Coast Guard station, Milwaukee, occupied by AIM in 1971 and used by the Milwaukee Indian Community School until 1981.

Courtesy of the Great Lakes Indian
Fish & Wildlife Commission

Above: Hundreds of treaty supporters merged with treaty protesters at the Butternut Lake landing (Ashland County) in 1987 following a Solidarity Rally at the Lac du Flambeau Reservation. The rally drew tribal members and supporters from across the country. Butternut Lake was the site of some of the first confrontations and harassment of treaty spear fishers and their families in 1985.

Left: Poster seen in bars in northern Wisconsin during the height of the spear fishing controversy.

Photo courtesy of Potawatomi Bingo Casino

Potawatomi Bingo Casino, an enterprise of the Forest County Potawatomi Tribe, is located close to downtown Milwaukee in the Menominee River Valley. It has become an important component in the city's long-range plan of renewal and beautification to serve commercial, light manufacturing, residential, and recreational purposes in a once heavily industrialized area. The enterprise began in 1991 as a joint effort to generate funding to support both the tribe in Forest County and the intertribal Indian Community School in Milwaukee. The school and gaming properties were acquired by the Forest County Potawatomi as part of their reservation and are under federal jurisdiction. The facility was greatly expanded and its functions diversified with an addition opened November 1, 2001. Besides gaming — bingo, video and reel slot machines, and blackjack — the Potawatomi Bingo Casino now includes a large parking structure, three restaurants, cabaret-style theater entertainment featuring nationally known performers, a gift shop and convenience store, and a conference center. The décor throughout features Potawatomi cultural themes and motifs. Employing nearly 1,500 people — the majority non-Indian — Potawatomi Bingo Casino, like other tribes' gaming establishments throughout the state, is a tremendous economic asset to the local economy.

Ho-Chunk bison herd near Muscoda.

Indian Summer Festival, held at Milwaukee's Maier Park on the weekend following Labor Day, attracts Indian participants from all over the country as well as people from local tribes.

Contest dancing in the young men's traditional category, annual Ho-Chunk Labor Day Weekend Powwow, Black River Falls.

Powwow, an eastern Algonkian word for religious leaders and the rituals they performed, was adopted into English by whites in the eighteenth century to describe a noisy, usually political, gathering. By the end of the nineteenth century it gained currency among whites to describe hired performances of Indian dancing and singing before paying audiences. Indian people on the Plains probably were the first to adopt the term for their own social gatherings to sing and dance. Powwows proliferated across the country, especially during the relocation program of the 1950s, as distinctively *Indian* affairs. Although standardized in basic format, powwows are part of a dynamic, living tradition: drum groups add newly composed or borrowed songs to their repertoires; fashions and fads in apparel (called "outfits," not "costumes") come and go; and special activities associated with the powwow scene vary by region or tribe — giveaways, games, memorial meals, and the nature of foods and the kinds of items sold at stands ringing the dance arena.

Dance sessions open with a "Grand Entry" led by flag bearers, a carry-over from the old rodeos and wild west shows where Indians found careers and learned "show biz" well before the beginning of the twentieth century. Successive groups of

Myrtle Thunder Long, traditional dancer. The number on the shawl she carries is typical of identification used in judging at contest powwows. Although Ho-Chunk, Mrs. Long is wearing a traditional Plains style outfit.

Photo courtesy of Paul Arentz, *Hocak Worak*

dancers enter the dance arena according to gender, dance category (identifiable by the style of a dancer's outfit), and age, from "seniors" to "tiny tots." Strict protocol regulates the order of "host" and "visitor" drum groups' performances. A good M.C. with a sense of humor is essential to announce events, explain things for non-Indian visitors, and maintain a friendly mood.

Though they share the same basic format, there are two distinct kinds of powwow: traditional and contest. Contest powwows, typically larger than traditional powwows, have become increasingly popular since the end of World War II. They are scheduled and advertised well in advance. Their central feature is formally judged dance competitions; these are interspersed with a few noncompetitive "intertribals" when anyone can dance. Traditional powwows are purely social events, often to honor a person or occasion — birthdays, graduations, national holidays ("sobriety powwows" have become widely popular New Years' Eve celebrations), or anniversaries of important events in a tribe's history.

Photo courtesy of Al Gedicks

Protection of waterways is a major issue in the opposition to the proposed zinc/copper mine near Crandon (Forest County).

Photo courtesy of Al Gedicks

Indians and non-Indians united in protest against the Crandon mine, state capitol building, Madison.

❧ 8 ❧

CHIPPEWA TREATY RIGHTS CONTROVERSY

While the Menominees were still demonstrating for the repeal of their termination in 1971, the Lac Courte Oreilles (LCO) Chippewas occupied a dam site of the Northern States Power Company near Winter in Sawyer County to protest the renewal of the company's fifty-year lease to maintain the dam. When the company built the dam in 1921, it did not move Indian graves and homes as promised in the contract. The dam also flooded much more of the reservation than the contract stipulated, doing great environmental damage and destroying wild rice beds the Indians depended on for food and income. The LCO occupiers withdrew in a few days on a plea from Governor Lucey.

After more than a decade of annual renewals of the lease, litigation, and negotiation, the company and the LCO reached a creative and amicable resolution of the issue. The power company, now Excel Energy, extended to the tribe a large, long-term loan to construct and manage a power plant, LCO Hydro/Electric, at the west end of Winter Dam. The plant supplies energy far beyond the reservation's borders. The profits go to retire the loan; when the loan is paid off, profits will accrue to the tribe. The Winter Dam case was an earnest of Chippewa activism to come.

During the 1950s and 1960s, when tribes across the country cried out against the abrogation of treaties with regard to termination and taking of reservation land for dams and other purposes, a good many lawyers considered treaties a forlorn hope as grounds for suit. This is no longer the case, as the legal profession has had to take a new and careful look at old treaties. A precedent-setting case in 1974 in the state of Washington had special importance for the Wisconsin Chippewas. The treaties in Washington contained a provision that the tribes there could continue to fish in the territory they ceded. When they tried to exercise their rights, the state of Washington, spurred by anti-Indian agitators, opposed them. The case went to the U.S. District Court, where Judge Boldt found in favor of the Indians in 1974, a decision upheld by the U.S. Circuit Court of Appeals and the U.S. Supreme Court (which declined to review it). After all the years of rancor over the Boldt decision, Washington State government rethought its position; it now works closely with the tribes on cooperative programs for resource management.

The Chippewa treaties allowed them to hunt, fish, and gather in the areas they ceded in 1837 and 1842 until they would be moved to reservations in Minnesota; these rights were not extinguished in the 1854 treaty, which established Chippewa reservations in Wisconsin. Wild rice lakes and stands of sugar maple trees were important sources of subsistence to the Chippewas, who also gathered berries, medicines, and other plant products for various purposes on the ceded land; however, unlike hunting and fishing, gathering went largely unnoticed and unchallenged. Since the beginning of the twentieth century, the state of Wisconsin tried to enforce its fish and game regulations not only in the ceded areas but on the reservations themselves, on the theory that Indian treaty rights were automatically canceled when Wisconsin became a state in 1848. The courts were not entirely consistent on this contention over the years but in 1931 established that the state did not have jurisdiction to enforce game laws on the reservations.

The off-reservation issue remained more or less moot until after World War II. When the sudden growth of tourism by the 1950s brought enormous numbers of visitors to hunt and especially to fish in northern Wisconsin, the state increased patrolling to make sure the visitors paid for game licenses. Game wardens became aware that Indians were still hunting and fishing in the ceded areas, even out of season, and were using illegal methods such as gill nets and spears. With the passage of PL 280 in 1953 giving jurisdiction for law and order over reservations in Wisconsin, the state cracked down on Indians both on and off the reservations in regard to game laws. Again the Indians protested, and in 1966 the state attorney general ruled that the state could enforce its game laws on Indians only outside the boundaries of reservations.

As the tribes began turning to the courts for redress, the legal profession took greater interest in Indian law, and the subject began appearing in law schools' curricula. Indian treaties, it turned out, still carried weight, and the Supreme Court, at least in theory, had tried to give the Indians a fair shake. After the government stopped making treaties with Indian tribes in 1871, the treaties that had been made remained in force, although under special circumstances and with cause the United States might end specific provisions in a given treaty.

As the U.S. Supreme Court began hearing treaty-related cases in the late nineteenth and early twentieth centuries, questions of meaning and intent arose, requiring interpretation. Besides the universal difficulties of translation between any two languages, some treaties had to go through several Indian languages and sometimes even French before the tribe concerned and the Federal representatives could communicate. The Supreme Court also recognized that the Indians did not bargain from a position of strength like that of the United States. These circumstances gave rise to four canons, or principles, in resolving equivocal meanings. Briefly, treaties must be construed liberally as a whole in the Indians' favor as must any ambiguous expressions in or relating to treaties, and, as far as it can be determined, treaties must be construed as the Indians would have understood them at the time they were negotiated. Finally, if the United States extinguished a treaty right, it could not have done so for merely implied reasons but rather by explicit action and the use of "clear and plain" language.

These canons were not widely known or used until the 1970s, because until that time not many treaty cases reached the Supreme Court (or any court, for that matter) and few lawyers were sufficiently versed in Indian law to appreciate their significance. A wake-up case occurred in 1962, when a Menominee Indian was arrested for hunting out of season in Menominee County, the former reservation. The case moved from court to court on appeal. The state of Wisconsin argued that treaty rights no longer applied since the tribe had been terminated; the defendant's attorneys argued that if this were true, then the Menominee tribe had been deprived of a precious right and were owed compensation. The case eventually reached the U.S. Supreme Court, which ruled in 1967 that since the termination legislation had not said explicitly that hunting rights were extinguished on the former reservation, these rights still held. This same logic allowed the Menominees to sue successfully after restoration for damages incurred during termination, including payment of state taxes. Taxation came by implication with the termination plan and county status, but the Menominee Termination Act had not explicitly extinguished the exemption from state taxation inherent in reservation status.

In the early 1970s the Bad River and Red Cliff Chippewas successfully pursued treaty right litigation allowing them to fish in Lake Superior without regulation, but the famously controversial Chippewa fishing rights cases got underway in March 1974, when two brothers from LCO were arrested, charged, and found guilty for spear fishing off the reservation on Chief Lake in Sawyer County. The LCO Band brought suit against Lester P. Voigt, Secretary of the Department of Natural Resources, and other DNR and Sawyer County officials for interfering with Chippewa hunting and fishing rights. Federal District Court Judge James Doyle ruled against the LCO band in 1978. He did not rule that off-reservation treaty rights had been extinguished with the creation of the reservations, an argument that would be raised repeatedly and countered with evidence to the contrary in subsequent litigation, but his understanding was that any off-reservation fishing had to be confined to ceded lands adjacent to the reservation. The LCO Band went to the U.S. Court of Appeals for the Seventh Circuit, which reversed Doyle, and the U.S. Supreme Court declined to review the reversal in 1983. The reversal of the Doyle decision called for further court proceedings that Judge Doyle divided into three phases, in which the other five Chippewa bands joined with LCO as parties to the same treaties.

The first, "declaratory" phase was to determine the nature and scope of Chippewa treaty rights. Judge Doyle decided this issue liberally in February of 1987, reflecting the Supreme Court's canons, having determined that the Chippewas understood hunting and fishing to mean the commercial sale of fish and all the methods and equipment they might employ. Opponents of this decision argue that the treaty meant the use of "primitive" or "aboriginal" means of fishing for subsistence, but by the early nineteenth century the Chippewa were already long accustomed to selling fish and using new equipment such as metal spears and nets of commercial twine rather than willow bark cordage, and they were hunting with guns and metal traps.

The second, "regulatory" phase of the proceedings was to determine the permissible scope of regulation by the state of Wisconsin in view of the fact that the landscape, ownership, and distribution of species had changed in the ceded area. After Doyle's death in 1987, he was succeeded by Judge Barbara Crabb who handed down five decisions between 1987 and 1991 in the spirit of the 1987 Doyle decision. In 1987 Crabb decided in favor of tribal self-regulation except where there might be a risk to public health and safety, at which time the state could regulate as long as it "does not discriminate against the Indians." Crabb's 1988 and 1989 decisions concerned fish harvest limits and were favorable to the Indians, as was the 1990 decision about deer hunting and trapping of small game and furbearers. In 1991 Crabb ruled that the term *usual privileges of occupancy* (in the 1842 treaty) related to forest products such as maple sap, birch bark, firewood, and the like and did not reserve the right to harvest timber commercially since it was not a Chippewa occupation at the time of the treaties. Both the Chippewas and the state of Wisconsin had the right to appeal within two months, on any of the phases, but neither party chose to do so.

The third, "damages" phase was to determine the amount of damages, if any, the Chippewas were entitled to for interference in their treaty rights. In 1990 Crabb reluctantly ruled against damages insofar as technically it would require the federal government, which made the treaties, to join the suit on behalf of the Chippewas against the state of Wisconsin, which had interfered with the Indians' treaty rights. The Chippewas' appeal was pending before the Supreme Court in 1991 when the six bands withdrew it "as a gesture of peace and friendship towards the people of Wisconsin, in a spirit they hope may someday be reciprocated on the part of the general citizenry and officials of this state."

That the Chippewas would take this stand is astonishing, considering all that had led up to it. In 1983 Tony Earl, a former head of the DNR and governor of Wisconsin, had officially called for cooperation between the tribal governments and state agencies, but the state continued to oppose the Chippewa bands in court, vociferously supported by the kind of anti-Indian groups that opposed the tribes in Washington State on the grounds that Indian treaty rights and tribal sovereignty were discriminatory to white Americans and the treaties were too old to be an issue in the late 1900s. They were joined by some sports hunters and fishers and resort owners who believed their propaganda claiming that the Indians would harvest all the fish and game in the state and destroy the tourist industry. These organizations favor names that sound fair minded, patriotic, and conservation oriented. Along with ICERR (Interstate Congress for Equal Rights and Responsibilities, founded in the West in 1976), home-grown groups arose such as WARR (Wisconsin Alliance for Rights and Resources), PARR (Protect Americans' Rights and Resources), and STA (Stop Treaty Abuse, Inc.). These groups helped to defeat Earl in the 1986 gubernatorial race, when Tommy Thompson came out against the decision upholding treaty rights to hunt and fish. When the 1987 decision was made public and Indians resumed spearing fish in ceded territory, their outraged opponents showed up at boat landings to harass, insult, and physically threaten them. They spread groundless rumors of great piles of fish and game the Indians killed just for fun and left to rot, and other baseless atrocity stories.

The Lac du Flambeau people were the most active in asserting treaty rights and formed the Waswagon Treaty Organization to unite the Chippewas in their common cause early in the course of the controversy. Although spearfishing occurred in a number of places in the ceded areas, the greatest volume of fish were taken from lakes in the environs of the Lac du Flambeau Reservation, and the most threatening and violent anti-Indian demonstrations took place there.

In 1984 the Chippewas established the Great Lakes Indian Fish and Wildlife Commission (GLIFWC) to education the public about the facts at issue and to work with state agencies in developing their own criteria to regulate seasons, locations, and "safe harvest" limits. The concept of safe harvests entails an annual process by which the state DNR and the GLIFWC survey fish populations and agree on the total number of fish available from individual lakes without threatening the species; the Indians are allowed only a portion of that amount. Opponents of Indian spear fishing interpreted this as one-sided, favoring the Indians, but the tribes have never taken the full amount they are entitled to under the safe harvest formula. Furthermore, Indian fishers are subject to an exact count of all fish taken by spearing, while non-Indian anglers operate on a loosely enforced bag limit. Besides the Wisconsin Chippewas, GLIFWC includes the Chippewa groups in Minnesota and Michigan whose usufructuary rights to hunt, fish, and gather in ceded areas were also covered in their treaties. Their experiences with litigation paralleled the Wisconsin situation, and they too were harassed by hate groups.

The Chippewas' problems soon attracted positive intertribal and non-Indian support from established civil rights and conservation groups and those that sprang up to counter the likes of ICERR, PARR, and the rest. Working with Waswagon and other Chippewa organizations, they came to the boat landings as witnesses. Beyond that, they helped to counter inflammatory rumor mongering and educate the public about treaties and other Indian issues through lectures, seminars, and publications. HONOR (Honor Our Neighbors Origins and Rights) began in response to the treaty controversy in Wisconsin and by 1988 had evolved into a national activist organization that continues to monitor and publish on Indian affairs. The largely non-Indian Midwest Treaty Network, modeled after the Witnesses for Peace organization in Central America, joined with HONOR in witnessing at the boat landings.

Since the Chippewas decided that their rights had finally been secured and they would not seek damages, there has been a florescence of cooperative resource management and joint efforts with the DNR and other state agencies. As people in northern Wisconsin realized that the prophesies of doom had not materialized and that the non-Indians' demonstrations constituted the real threat to tourism and the resort industry, the Indian spear fishing season calmed down. Although it is still not widely publicized, the Chippewa bands maintain fish hatcheries, a legacy of the Collier administration going back to the 1930s, and stock their lakes and streams. More than 90 percent of these fish are caught by non-Indian sports fishers.

An unusual variation on the question of Indian hunting concerns the Wisconsin Winnebagos, who have no treaty setting aside a reservation where they have the right to hunt. Their traditional religion requires venison at ritual feasts, but from the time the state of Wisconsin enacted game laws in the early 1900s Winnebago men often were arrested for hunting out of season. By quiet persuasion, the Winnebago tribe gained the full cooperation of the Department of Natural Resources (DNR) when it was still headed by Tony Earl and were able to get a bill passed in the Wisconsin legislature in 1978 allowing them to hunt as needed for religious purposes. Tribal elders drew up restrictions in the bill requiring that they give advance notice to the DNR as to time, place, names of hunters, and expected harvest to prevent anyone using religion as an excuse for poaching.

❧ 9 ❧

MINING AND
WISCONSIN INDIAN LANDS

In 1975 the Exxon Corporation discovered a zinc-copper sulfide deposit in Forest County in an area including part of the Mole Lake Chippewa Reservation. The region was economically depressed, and neighboring white landowners jumped at the first offers of contracts to explore for minerals, but the Indians argued and debated among themselves and retained a mining consultant to advise them. They concluded that the harm a mine would do to their homeland far outweighed any economic benefits and would have undesirable effects for the whole region. By the early 1980s many non-Indians in the area shared the Indians' opinion. Exxon withdrew from the project in the face of mounting opposition and a drop in metal prices, but the corporation returned in 1993 in partnership with Rio Algom of Canada, which quickly encountered an even more determined opposition, with Indians and non-Indians presenting a united front.

By this time Indian casinos were beginning to show profits to pay for research and litigation and were on the way to becoming major employers in many northern counties, benefiting non-Indians as well as the tribes. Even sports fishing enthusiasts who had once opposed the Chippewas' treaty rights realized that mining could ruin fishing for everyone. Opponents of the Crandon mine commissioned studies that revealed that the proposed mine would generate sulfuric acid wastes and use enormous quantities of cyanide and other toxic chemicals to process the ore. The mine also would require so much water that it would lower the groundwater tables in the region. The largest toxic waste dump in the state's history would be located at the headwaters of the Wolf River. The mining companies denied the results of their opponents' studies and brought underhanded efforts to bear. In December of 1996 the town board of the township of Nashville (which includes the Mole Lake Reservation) signed a mining agreement with Exxon/Rio Algom after closed-door meetings and over the objections of the majority of residents. A completely new board, including a Mole Lake tribal member, was voted into office in the April 1997 election. They rescinded the agreement, holding up issuance of a mining permit from the state.

The mineral deposit lies about a mile upstream from the Mole Lake Chippewas' wild rice beds, which have economic value for home consumption and sale and tremendous sacred significance to all the Chippewa people as a special gift of the Creator. The Forest County Potawatomi Reservation is only a few miles away from the deposit, and the Menominee Reservation is located about forty miles downstream along the Wolf River. The Stockbridge-Munsee Reservation adjoins the Menominee Reservation. The Mole Lake, Potawatomi, Menominee, and Stockbridge-Munsee formed an intertribal council to monitor the mining companies' activities; they were soon joined by the Lac du Flambeau Chippewas, whose reservation lies to the west, and the Oneidas, whose reservation is located southeast of the Menominee and Stockbridge Reservations.

When the Clean Air and Clean Water Acts of the 1970s were amended to include tribal lands, the Mole Lake Chippewa tribe applied to the U.S. Environmental Protection Agency (EPA) in 1995 for "Treatment-as-State" status under the Clean Water Act, giving them the authority to regulate water quality on their reservation and authority over discharges from upstream industrial and municipal facilities. The Wisconsin attorney general, James E. Doyle, immediately sued the EPA and the tribe in federal court, demanding that the federal government reverse the EPA's approval of the Mole Lake Chippewas' regulatory powers. Chippewa supporters circulated a petition urging the state to drop the suit; it was signed by more than two dozen environmental groups, two townships in the area, and more than 450 people from communities all over Wisconsin. In the spring of 1999 the U.S. District Court in Milwaukee dismissed the suit on the basis of a long and careful review of the facts; the state immediately entered an appeal. Meanwhile, four more townships downstream from the proposed mine had registered their support of EPA and the tribe.

When the state of Wisconsin exercised its option of appeal to a higher court, various Indian and non-Indian coalitions mounted educational campaigns, buying space in newspapers in northern Wisconsin, arranging discussion meetings and lectures, and communicating via the Internet and e-mail. They also are opposed to the high-voltage lines needed to power the mine, which are seen as a threat to farmers and others across northwestern Wisconsin. Other Indian groups in the state entered amicus briefs in support of the Mole Lake Chippewas in the pending suit.

On September 21, 2001, the Seventh Circuit Court of Appeals in Chicago ruled that the EPA can allow the Sakaogon (Mole Lake) Chippewa band to regulate waters affecting their reservation because their survival depends on this resource. The Court also rejected the state's contention that since stream beds are inarguably state land and under its jurisdiction, this would include waters in the streams; the Court noted precedents in other cases recognizing instances of "overlapping jurisdictions." While rejoicing in this victory, the matter is not fully settled as of this writing. The state exercised the option of requesting the Seventh Circuit Court of Appeals to review its decision, and the matter is still pending as of late 2001. If the Court still finds in favor of the EPA and Mole Lake Chippewa, the state can take its case to the U.S. Supreme Court. On the other hand, if the Seventh Circuit Court should reverse its original decision, undoubtedly the EPA and Mole Lake will appeal to the Supreme Court.

Although the foregoing developments stop the mine at present, the mining interests have not abandoned their efforts. In 1998 the state legislature passed a moratorium on mining until mining companies can show a single example of a safe metallic sulfide mine anywhere in North America. While such evidence has not been forthcoming, spokespersons for the industry express confidence that they can overcome this hurdle.

Beyond a local pro-mining minority and a number of Wisconsin businesses with a stake in promoting the Crandon mine, there also are powerful interests supporting the mine that are totally removed from and indifferent to any considerations but profit. Exxon recognized the risk to its image as an American company and saw the wisdom of pulling out of the deal. In 2000 Billiton, a London-based South African company, purchased Exxon's Canadian partner, Rio Algom. In its national and international publications, the mining industry has taken note of Wisconsin as one of its major battlegrounds.

As Indians and concerned non-Indians face a common threat, non-Indians are beginning to understand they too can benefit from the Indians' long-standing insistence on respect for treaty rights and tribal sovereignty to protect the land. The federal recognition of Chippewa treaty rights in the ceded lands in the Doyle/Crabb decisions gave the tribes what the law calls legal standing to present cases in federal courts to challenge mining companies. Although the treaties do not cover mineral rights, there is a potential argument that degradation of off-reservation resources would be an "environmental violation" of treaty rights.

❧ 10 ❧

SOVEREIGNTY, RECOGNITION, GAMING, AND BEYOND

The growing realization in Congress during the 1960s that the termination policy was unworkable and inhumane led in the 1970s to a changed philosophy about Indian affairs and legislative action that was sensitive to tribal interests. In January of 1975 Congress created the American Indian Policy Review Commission, which submitted its two-volume Final Report in May of 1977. The ten-member Commission, chaired by Senator James Abourezk (D South Dakota) with Congressman Lloyd Meeds (R Washington) as vice chairman, was made up of five members of Congress and five Indians, including Ada Deer from Wisconsin (the only woman) and Adolph Dial, a member of the unrecognized Lumbee tribe of North Carolina. Ernest L. Stevens, a Wisconsin Oneida, directed the Commission's executive staff of well over one hundred people (the vast majority of them Indians) who did the legwork. The staff produced dozens of reports reviewing and recommending policy. These publications are very useful reference works, but policy changes and much of the new legislation had actually occurred or were under way before the Commission's Final Report appeared.

Congress passed the Indian Self-Determination and Education Assistance Act in 1975 and restored some of the features that had been cut out of the Indian Reorganization Act of 1934. Although implementation is not automatic but on a tribe-by-tribe basis, it allows tribes that qualify to administer their own federal services programs: operation of schools, health clinics, job training, and welfare programs, to mention only some of the services supported by federal and tribal funds. The Act was amended in 1988, under the title Self Governance, to expedite its operation by cutting down further on requirements of federal supervision. The Oneida is the only tribe in Wisconsin operating under the amended Act.

A controversial issue in the Review Commission's report was the recommendation that tribes not served by the federal government be allowed to apply for recognition. Congressman Meeds was so opposed to letting any more tribes under the federal umbrella that he entered a minority statement of disagreement that some readers interpret as based solely on economic grounds. The rest of the commissioners considered it unconscionable to perpetuate injustices and inequities that were accidents of history. In 1978 the BIA Branch of Acknowledgement and Research (BAR) was established with teams of genealogists, historians, and anthropologists to review tribes' applications to determine whether they qualify for federal recognition. BAR has been criticized since its inception for its excessive slowness, technical hairsplitting, unnecessarily burdensome demands on the applicants, and inconsistent decisions about the documentation tribes must submit to fulfill four basic requirements. These are to establish their history, tribal organization, membership, and "external identification" as an Indian entity since 1900 such as state recognition. The process is costly for the tribes and takes about ten years for a tribe to complete. More than two hundred groups expressed interest in applying when BAR began its work; as of 2001 BAR had decided only thirty cases and has twenty-five completed applications before it to review. The Brothertown tribe of Wisconsin stands fourth in line as of 2001.

While the Indian Self-Determination Act was passed with the explicit intent of helping tribes pull themselves out of poverty, and there was a real sense of prosperity during the 1970s, it was the familiar case of the government trying to solve problems by just throwing money at them. Most tribes were dependent on the federal government and had to apply for short-term funding for specific and finite programs, following guidelines out of Washington rather than having the latitude to develop their own plans. They got very good at grantsmanship, but there was no capitalization for long-term investment or income-generating projects or, in some cases, even renewal of essential programs. When the money began to peter out, even before the election of President Ronald Reagan, the tribes were no better off.

Casting about for solutions, the chair of the South Florida Seminoles, James Billie, observed that many states were turning to gaming, particularly lotteries, to raise revenue. The tribe, like many others, already had a "smoke shop" selling cut-rate cigarettes on the reservation, where they do not have to charge state taxes. In 1979 Billie consulted a lawyer, who confirmed the logic of Billie's idea that state regulations setting the size of payoffs and hours of operation on church bingo games did not apply to the reservation. A large crowd turned out the evening Seminole Reservation Bingo opened, thanks to the tribe's widespread advertising of high stakes and unrestricted hours. It was just as quickly closed down by the Florida Attorney General Robert Butterworth, but not for long. Billie's lawyer went to federal court and got a quick ruling *(Seminole Tribe v. Butterworth, Florida, 1979)*: since bingo was a legal activity within the state of Florida, the Seminoles' federally recognized sovereignty entitled them to regulate their own bingo games played on federal reservation land. The case was so unusual that it attracted a lot of publicity, and word spread quickly throughout Indian Country. Bingo halls began springing up in states where gaming of any kind was permitted.

Although Indian Bingo began after BAR was established, and tribes were beginning work on their applications before bingo gave rise to large-scale gaming, the anti-Indian sovereignty interpretation is that the desire to cash in on Indian gaming gave rise to BAR. But not all the tribes seeking recognition are located in areas where Indian gaming is permitted. Even the spectacularly lucrative Foxwoods Casino of the Mashantucket Pequots in Connecticut was the unexpected outcome of the tribe's successful application for federal recognition, not to BAR, but through an Act of Congress. A tribe member, Richard Haywood, at his grandmother's urging, began casting about as early as 1972 for a means of saving their little Pequot reservation, which would revert to the state when the last resident, his grandmother, died.

Because Indian gaming is not only unregulated but untaxed by the state in which it is located, state governments were unhappy to be deprived of revenue and went to court. Another landmark federal court ruling *(California v. Cabazon Band, 1987)* reinforced the legal theory that since neither the states nor the federal government are subject to suit or taxation, the tribes' sovereign status confers similar immunity. It is important, however, to dispel the impression that all the tribes are benefiting enormously from gaming. Of the more the 557 currently recognized tribes, fewer than a third are able to avail themselves of gaming because their federal land lies within states that do not permit any kind of gambling. And very few of the tribes involved in gaming are turning huge profits because of the isolated location of reservations, far from large population centers to draw upon for their clientele. Nevertheless, this successful test of tribal sovereignty holds the potential of other possibilities where gaming is not an option.

The Wisconsin tribes happen to be excellently situated. The state runs lotteries and allows churches and other nonprofit organizations to offer bingo for fund raising, and there is relatively easy access to the reservations from large urban areas — Milwaukee, Madison, Green Bay, Chicago, and the Twin Cities. Gaming took off in Wisconsin in the early 1980s, with the Oneidas opening the first bingo hall and the other tribes soon following suit. Tribes engaged in bingo were soon testing the waters for other gaming opportunities and, in 1985, formed the National Indian Gaming Association (NIGA) as a nonprofit intertribal organization to assist tribes with their gaming enterprises and protect them from states' efforts to tax them. There were rumors from the start that Indian gaming was controlled by organized crime, because the tribes usually needed investors to get their gaming operations going. Certainly there were opportunists who tried to exploit the Indians, but information exchanged through NIGA and other intertribal agencies helped weed out shady deals.

Congress, however, passed the Indian Gaming Regulatory Act (IGRA) in 1988, setting up classes of gambling from bingo to casino games with different degrees of required federal/state regulation. Supposedly intended to protect the tribes from infiltration by mobsters, IGRA really facilitated the states' getting what many people consider nothing but payola in lieu of taxes from compacts the tribes must negotiate with the states to operate casinos. In Wisconsin, compacts apply to specified periods of years and then must be re-negotiated.

In Wisconsin, casinos have been added to the original bingo operations on the six Chippewa reservations and on the Oneida, Stockbridge-Munsee, and Menominee Reservations. The Stockbridge-Munsees' casino is on land restored to tribal trust status up to 1972, enabling them to buy back land in recent years for various kinds of economic development, including a golf course. As of this writing they are engaged in litigation with the state of Wisconsin, which opposes their opening a second casino on newly acquired land although it has been put in tribal trust. The widely scattered Ho-Chunk Nation has bingo-casino enterprises near Wisconsin Dells, Black River Falls, and Nekoosa; at Madison they offer only bingo. The Ho-Chunks acquired practically all of their tribal land trust after 1963, a small percentage of it specifically for gaming enterprises. The Potawatomis operate a casino in Forest County, but their major gaming is Potawatomi Bingo Casino in Milwaukee, where they bought land and put it in tribal trust status.

When high stakes bingo was first planned to support the Indian Community School in Milwaukee, there were protests from some church groups and other organizations that it would wipe out their state-regulated games. The Potawatomis set up a fund to compensate such groups if they could show from receipts that over the course of a year their bingo income had declined. The fund was never tapped. Recalling their earlier disadvantage when gaming began for the Wisconsin tribes, the Potawatomis have extended assistance to the equally isolated Red Cliff Chippewas.

Inspired by Las Vegas and other major gaming areas, the Indian casinos are also entertainment centers featuring nationally known performers, from rock bands to wrestlers, and advertised on prime-time TV and in newspapers. Besides a wide selection of dining facilities, luxury hotels have become part of the bingo casino complexes. Where gaming is successful, as in Wisconsin, it has raised tribal living standards, providing funding for everything from housing (emphasizing the needs of the elderly first) to clinics and educational programs, but even here it will take a long time before the tribes can fully rectify the economically depressed conditions in Indian communities for rational community development due to the loss and fragmentation of their land. Because gaming is such a labor-intensive industry, it provides employment to many more non-Indians than Indians; this is the real but unsung reason for the economic improvement over the past few years in the state's poorest counties.

Also generally not known is that gaming accounts for generous tribal contributions to worthy causes that are not exclusively Indian: local chapters of heart, cancer, Make-A-Wish and other health-related foundations as well as a host of environmental and cultural organizations. The Wisconsin tribes, like Indians across the country, responded sympathetically and generously to the terrorist tragedy of September 11, 2001, observing the "Day of Mourning" and sending volunteers and donations to help in the recovery efforts.

The Wisconsin tribes also recognize the need for economic diversification in the event that gaming does not remain popular. They are exploring, experimenting, and investing in a host of new enterprises such as golf courses and other recreational facilities, service stations with convenience stores and other retailing, light industries, specialized crops such as cranberries, and animal husbandry such as the Winnebagos' buffalo herd and the Forest County Potawatomis' herd of domesticated European deer. Some efforts have failed, others show promise, and some are succeeding, but gaming has provided capital for necessary, though sometimes disappointing, learning experiences.

The 1990s began with a major piece of legislation, the Native American Graves Protection and Repatriation Act (NAGPRA). Desecration of the dead has been a bitter issue for Indian people since robbing Indian graves was almost a cottage industry, as one historian put it, to supply the "science" of phrenology in the nineteenth century. Indians had other concerns, particularly questions about the circumstances underlying the acquisition of sacred objects and their public display. Although NAGPRA grew out of genuine instances of questionable and disrespectful practices across the country, the legislation created a confrontational climate when Indian people and museums were developing positive working relationships. In fact, in Wisconsin, people from all the tribes had long enjoyed visiting and working with the personnel at the Milwaukee Public Museum, the Wisconsin Historical Society in Madison, archeological research centers, and similar institutions.

NAGPRA applies only to museums and other depositories that receive or have received any federal funding. (Private collectors and dealers are exempt.) They must develop inventories and notify any tribes whose objects are in their collections so the tribes can decide whether to request repatriation. NAGPRA can only be adverted to here; it would require a separate publication to deal with the controversies in developing the legislation and the complicated procedures entailed in trying to implement it. Indian people who are trying to establish tribal museums or engage in archeological research are becoming aware that NAGPRA is not a cure-all for Indian grievances with "the white man" and are as concerned as their non-Indian counterparts about its possibly chilling effects on future study of American Indian history and culture. But NAGPRA has great symbolic utility. Generally, when it became law in 1990, non-Indians who heard about it were uncritically supportive; it is an easy conscience-soother about "what we did to the poor Indians," whatever it was.

The rise of Indian gaming, however, has evoked old antagonisms that Indians are getting "special privileges." The complaints play on widespread public misunderstanding that confuses Indians as a "racial" minority group of individual persons, with Indian tribes having constitutionally recognized sovereignty comparable, though not identical, to that of states, and much older. Senator Slade Gorton (R Washington) in 1997 and 1998 tried to introduce legislation to undercut tribal sovereignty by, among other things, calling for a means test for federal funding, especially if tribes had gaming, and abolishing tribes' immunity to suit. Predictably, he titled his bill the "American Indian Equal Justice Act." The bill had to be withdrawn when the Supreme Court ruled in 1998 that a lender could not sue the Kiowa tribe for a loan on which the tribe had defaulted. Neither states nor the federal government can be sued unless a contractor obtains a waiver of immunity in a given transaction, and the same applies to tribes. Gorton was defeated in his bid for reelection in 2000. Perhaps the people in Washington state learned something from the fishing controversies they too experienced in the 1970s, but there are antisovereignty legislators in other states, and as tribes win a few rounds in the courts, the greater becomes the threat of white backlash.

It is difficult to say when the Indian rallying cry shifted from "Broken Treaties" to "Tribal Sovereignty," but it is related to the shift from reactive seeking redress of old grievances to proactive and innovative tribal endeavors such as gaming. Those who oppose the Indians try to dismiss tribal sovereignty as a new Indian gimmick, but tribal sovereignty figured in the AICC Declaration of Indian Purpose in 1961, which in turn adverted to its importance in legal decisions from the earliest days of the United States and the colonies before that. Some tribes don't have treaties with the United States, but the very fact that the United States made treaties with Indian tribes at all acknowledges their sovereignty.

❧ 11 ❧

EXPANDING HORIZONS

Two weeks after the Winter Dam occupation in 1971, the Milwaukee chapter of AIM occupied a vacant Coast Guard station on Milwaukee's lakefront, using the same treaty rationale put forward at Alcatraz. AIM's intention was to set up a multiservice center for Indians, and in fact an alcohol rehabilitation program did operate briefly on the property. What actually kept the Coast Guard station in Indian hands was the fact that two years prior to the occupation, several Indian mothers had begun a tutorial program in one of their homes for children who were truant or had dropped out of school. As more Indian parents wanted to enroll their children in this program, which included both academic help and emphasis on pride in Indian identity, the group obtained space in the basement of an inner-city church in 1970. According to local news stories at the time, it was the nation's first urban Indian school. Such schools soon sprang up in many cities across the country. The Indian Community School (ICS) in Milwaukee had outgrown its first location in less than a year, so when AIM occupied the Coast Guard station, the school's director moved the children in on AIM's heels; within about three years the school took the building over entirely from AIM.

The city did not want to become involved in a squabble over federal land, the Coast Guard did not want to provoke an incident where children were concerned, and the Interior Department, although concerned with Indian Bureau schools, was not eager to request transfer of jurisdiction over property belonging to another federal agency. The school remained open more or less by default and was supported by private donations and federal grants. Operated with a professional Indian and non-Indian staff, it was accredited and developed working relationships with the University of Wisconsin–Milwaukee School of Education.

When part of the Caravan of Broken Treaties passed through Milwaukee in 1972 on its way to the massive demonstration in Washington, D.C., that led to trashing the BIA building, some participants stayed overnight in the space AIM still used at the old Coast Guard Station. National and international coverage surrounding this stopover, along with the previous year's publicity surrounding the occupation of the building, alerted people in Milwaukee to the sizeable Indian presence in their city. At that time the Indian population there was estimated at about four thousand; that meant there had to be several hundred Indian children in the Milwaukee schools besides the fifty or so squeezed in at the lakefront. In 1972 the Milwaukee Public Schools system, in cooperation with Indian parents, started the We Indians program. Staffed by Indian educators, the program offers extracurricular activities in neighborhood schools with high Indian enrollments to provide cultural support for Indian children and encourage crosscultural understanding for non-Indian children.

The disposition of the lakefront property was finally settled in 1981 when the Coast Guard gave it to Milwaukee on the condition that Milwaukee would provide substitute quarters for the school; the city then gave ICS the use of the vacant and deteriorating Bartlett Avenue School. However, the school was forced to close in 1983 because of severe cuts in federal funding for Indian education during the Reagan Administration. The board and friends of the school were prepared to raise funds by various means to operate the school, but their resources were not equal to the additional burden of having to bring the building up to code.

The new head of the school board turned for help to the Judicare attorney who had spearheaded the legal work in the Menominees' drive for restoration. He negotiated with the city to give full and clear title to the Bartlett Avenue property, which was well located for commercial development. Beginning in 1985, a number of interesting ecumenical developments and a lot of sweat equity from the Indian community got the school going again in 1987. After investigating several possibilities, the school board settled on the vacant campus of Concordia College on the city's near-west side. The property belonged to the Missouri Synod Lutheran Church, which had relocated the campus north of the city.

ICS had enough money from the sale of the Bartlett Avenue property for a down payment on the Concordia land. The Lutherans offered generous terms, allowing the school to take immediate occupancy of the entire campus while paying it off in parcels on land contracts. Vagrants and vandals had gotten into several buildings and made an awful mess of them, windows were broken, and the grounds were littered with trash and grown over in weeds. The Indian community pitched in to rehabilitate the site.

There were some fine old houses in the neighborhood that had been or were in process of being restored, some even on the National Register of Historic Places. The owners and other area residents had expected that the campus would be sold to developers who would clear the property (some twelve acres and seven buildings) and build upscale apartments to transform a pretty run-down area. At this point the Catholic order of the Sisters of the Sorrowful Mother paid a commercial planning firm to come up with a development plan for adapting the newly acquired campus to the Indians' needs and generating income. Meanwhile, some of the nuns actually helped the Indians with the physical work — wiring, plumbing, and the like. The Wisconsin Electric company and other businesses contributed to the project.

The school was in desperate financial need and began a program to raise funds by making one of the buildings into low-income, elderly housing and renting dormitory space to Milwaukee Area Technical College students. But when the ICS reopened in 1987, there was barely enough cash even to run the place, let alone capitalize other moneymaking plans, and the school nearly had to close again. Coincidentally, all this was going on when Indian Bingo was taking off, and the school board planned to use some of the vacant land for a bingo facility. The school suddenly faced a fight on several fronts. While any school property was tax free, high-stakes Indian Bingo required that the property be tribal trust land.

The school approached various tribes, but they were busy getting into gaming on their reservations and distrusted the school's plan as competition. The Forest County Potawatomi, however, found they were at a disadvantage in developing a bingo facility. They lived far off the beaten tourist track, with several other tribes between them and potential bingo players, and they were the poorest of all the Wisconsin tribes. The tribe had a discontinuous reservation anyway, so extending their tribal trust status to property in Milwaukee seemed like a good idea.

It definitely did *not* seem like a good idea to some of the neighbors trying to gentrify the Concordia neighborhood and already unhappy about the Lutherans' sale of the campus to the Indians. They started a campaign claiming that Indian Bingo would attract both organized and local hoodlum crime, "because Indian Bingo winnings can be paid only in cash" (not true). Lawn signs protested, "No Reservation Here!" and even harsher sentiments. Informational meetings called by the school ended in the Indians enduring shouting and insults. Even when the school explained they had found an investor to buy property and build a gaming facility in the Menomonee River Valley, several miles from the campus, the anti-Indian neighbors continued to spread rumors and lobby the Common Council and County Board of Supervisors to oppose the Bingo hall to drive the Indians out. The city and county governments were worried that the Indians would not be subject to local building codes, but the school and the Potawatomi tribe signed a written agreement to abide by codes, making them subject to suit like any other property owner. On the other hand, some of the neighbors welcomed the ICS and did volunteer work for the school.

The school has gone through structural reorganization and leadership changes. The original profit sharing between the Potawatomi tribe and the school has been replaced with a buy-out of the school's interest over a period of years, investment income from this money to be used to maintain the school. ICS has bought a site of about 150 rural acres in the town of Franklin, south of Milwaukee, where a new school is to be built on an old farmstead site, leaving as much as possible of the land in a natural state.

In 1994 Spotted Eagle High School opened in one of the Concordia buildings but has its own board and is independent of the ICS. As an alternative and charter school funded by the Milwaukee Public School system for one hundred at-risk high school students (2001–2002 school year figure), it cannot serve only the Indian community; the student body is constituted at approximately half Indian and half non-Indian students.

A trend among reservations throughout the country is evident in Wisconsin, where tribes are forming their own school districts and electing their own school boards to administer and guide the curricula of their primary and high schools. There is a long tradition of tribally managed Head Start programs.

During the late 1960s the pattern in Wisconsin typified the national picture in higher education: increasing numbers of Indian students were seeking higher education but had a low graduation rate. Indian students themselves, along with concerned adults, approached college and university administrations to seek support services to help keep Indian students in school and develop programs in Indian studies and languages as well as hire Indian people in all disciplines. In many cases, the first efforts along these lines were met with the familiar attitude, spoken or implied, that Indians who went to college must be "assimilated" and didn't have problems or traditional cultural concerns needing special attention. Indian persistence paid off. These programs at various University of Wisconsin system campuses and private colleges are proving well justified.

Among the outcomes of the Policy Review Commission was the Tribally Controlled Community Colleges Act, which Congress passed in 1978. These schools are funded in part by the federal government through the BIA and various federal granting agencies, private foundations, and the tribes themselves. Vocational education funding for Indian youth also was made available. To date Wisconsin has two tribal colleges: one opened at the LCO Reservation in 1982, and the other opened at the Menominee Reservation in 1992. The College of the Menominee Nation is chartered by the Menominee people rather than the tribal government, as is usually the case. Enrollment is nearly 540 at Menominee and 600 at LCO, the latter figure including part-time as well as full-time students. Besides awarding two-year certificates in a variety of fields, these schools provide college experience in familiar surroundings to prepare students for completing four-year degrees elsewhere. Tribal community colleges welcome non-Indian students, thus serving educational needs beyond the boundaries of the reservations. There also are cooperative programs between a number of colleges and nearby reservations, such as one involving Northland College in Ashland and the Bad River Chippewa Reservation. The American Indian Educational Services, Inc., a private foundation based in Chicago, offers higher education at various sites around the country, including the Menominee Reservation.

Indian people in Milwaukee used various strategies to call attention to urban problems of housing, discriminatory treatment by law enforcement agencies, health needs, and other issues. Perhaps the greatest achievement amidst all the strident agitation and quiet pressure by Indian people in the 1970s was the federal government's gradual realization that it could not just forget Indians who lived in cities. In 1974 a group of concerned Indian people founded the Milwaukee Indian Health Center, now the Gerald L. Ignace Health Center, Inc., in response to serious health problems in the Indian community. Largely staffed by Indian people, it has encountered and prevailed over difficulties of funding, finding adequate facilities, and the need to revamp its organizational structure to meet changing circumstances in the field of public health.

Finally, among the various Indian institutions in Milwaukee, special mention must be made of Indian Summer Festivals, Inc. Throughout the summer weekends for many years, various ethnic festivals have been held at what is now called Maier Park on the city's lakefront. In September of 1987, the Indian community became part became of this tradition. The Indian group, eager to start a festival, began by consulting with the people responsible for well-established festivals such as Irish Fest and German Fest. These consultants gave the Indian organizers good advice: before starting a festival, hold off at least a year to raise enough money to withstand a whole weekend of bad weather and unexpected contingencies. They also advised the Indian group that as many people as possible should volunteer for a summer or more at the various ethnic festivals to learn the ropes and to adapt their interests to the lake front facilities, format, and regulations — folk dancing, concerts and other performances, vendors of different kinds of food and beverages, and sale of items ranging from souvenirs to high end art objects, all more or less representative of the ethnic group involved. Indian Summer added a great deal more in the way of educational demonstrations and insistence on authenticity than the other festivals (some of which are now following their lead). Because Indian Summer is held the weekend after Labor Day, it includes a Monday program for school groups. Of course, the Indian "folk dancing" is a huge weekend powwow, now the largest in the Midwest and drawing participants from throughout the state and all over the country.

✖ 12 ✖

SUMMING UP

Wisconsin has reflected, exemplified, and helped to shape national Indian policy. It has the distinction of having sent three people to Washington to head the Bureau of Indian Affairs: Philleo Nash, Robert Bennett, and, during President Clinton's administration, Ada Deer. It is among the half dozen or so states in which Indian gaming is a paying proposition, and people in Indian Country everywhere are watching what Wisconsin does. At present Washington is relatively sympathetic to the concept of tribal sovereignty, but the tribes, facing the combined power of the state and federal governments, have had to make concessions and compromises in their negotiations; this runs the risk of threatening tribal sovereignty and can sow political dissension within tribes concerning the competence and motives of their elected officers.

Everyone is not of the same mind in any group, no matter how harmonious. When the Menominees got their judgment in 1951, some tribal members opposed using any of the money for per capita payments and thought it should be added to their working capital. In retrospect, while the per capita money was soon spent, the people at least had the satisfaction of spending it; the carefully husbanded remainder disappeared in the debacle of termination.

Similarly, today all the Wisconsin tribes face decisions about what to do with gaming proceeds, and many are still so distrustful of the government that there is a clamor for more per capitas and other spending and less tying up of funds in investments for the future. With the suddenly unprecedented incomes from employment and per capitas, some Indian people fear that with the lure of consumer goods prosperity will do what poverty never could: assimilate them into mainstream America. Others

89

see an opportunity to use the white man's gadgets to the tribal advantage. For example, since the advent of TV two generations ago, there has been an alarming decline of speakers of the tribal languages. New methods of learning through computers and recorders offer hope of keeping the languages alive.

As globalization in the form of multinational extractive industries threatens the tribes, the tribes are going global. From local to national intertribal organizations, Indian people, representatives of Wisconsin tribes among them, are joining hands with other self-styled "First Peoples" of the world — Ainu in Japan, Australian Aborigines, New Zealand Maori, Saami in the Scandinavian countries, and others. Their problems turn out to be surprisingly similar, just as the problems faced by Indian peoples within this country turned out to be surprisingly similar — mines, dams, environmental degradation and destruction, land appropriation, and threats to self determination. Today these groups are exchanging strategies in an effort to survive with dignity and lead satisfying lives.

In 1980 I closed the account of *Wisconsin Indians* on a cautiously optimistic note. "The picture is much changed since the first version of this publication was issued in 1969. That it is generally brighter has been due to Indian efforts in their own behalf."

In 1969 the Menominee were still terminated and losing ground, literally, and tribes across the country still were afraid to assert themselves for fear of losing their land like the Menominee, who had been penalized for their success. I closed with a plea. "A cardinal premise of evolution, biological or cultural, is that variation is necessary to survival, so that when the environment becomes threatening there are variant forms fortuitously adapted to meet new challenges to perpetuate life. It can do no harm and might do us all a lot of good to hearken to what Indian people may have to tell us." Tribal sovereignty is a variant form, if you think about it.

REFERENCES AND RESOURCES

Indispensable Volumes for General Historical and Anthropological Reference

Cohen, Felix. *Handbook of Federal Indian Law*, Government Printing Office, 1942. Prepared under John Collier's administration to establish what power tribes really had in developing their IRA governments.

Kappler, Charles J., comp. & ed., *Indian Treaties 1778–1883*, Interland Publishing, Inc., New York, N.Y. 1972. Originally published for government use as *Indian Affairs: Laws and Treaties*, in two volumes in 1904, Volume II, *Treaties*, has been reprinted several times for general use and contains verbatim copies, including signers' names, of all ratified treaties and agreements that replaced treaties after 1871.

Prucha, Francis Paul. *The Great Father: The United States Government and the American Indians*, in two volumes, University of Nebraska Press, 1984. Prucha has published major reference works on many aspects of Indian affairs — treaty medals, boarding schools, self-appointed "friends of the Indians."

Royce, Charles C., comp., *Indian Land Cessions in the United States*, with an introduction by Cyrus Thomas, U.S. Bureau of American Ethnology, *Annual Report*, 1897 (Vol. 18, part 2), Smithsonian Institution, Washington, D.C., often referred to as "Royce and Thomas." The first half lists all the treaty and other cessions consecutively by date, identifies tribes, gives brief descriptions of the areas involved that are numbered and keyed to maps making up the second half of the volume.

Sturtevant, William C., gen. ed., *Handbook of North American Indians*, Vol. 15, *Northeast*, Bruce Trigger, ed., Smithsonian Institution, Washington, D.C., 1978. Includes concise ethnographies of all the tribes discussed here and throughout the area east to the Atlantic Ocean north of the Ohio River. Has excellent bibliographic documentation for each of the tribes for further reference. The volumes in the series cover other culture areas and general topics such as linguistics, Indian-white relations, and archeology.

RECENT ISSUES AND EVENTS

Chippewa Treaty Rights

Great Lakes Indian Fish and Wildlife Commission, *MASINAIGAN* (Muz in I ay gin) quarterly newspaper, covers news on the work of the Commission and its member tribes. Subscriptions are free; write *MASINAIGAN,* P.O. Box 9, Odanah, WI 54861.

Satz, Ronald N. *Chippewa Treaty Rights,* The Wisconsin Academy of Sciences, Arts, and Letters, Madison, WI, 1991.

Gaming

Eisler, Kim Isaac. *The Revenge of the Pequots,* Simon and Schuster, New York, NY, 2001. Besides dealing with the Pequot story, this well documented book details the start of Indian gaming among the Seminole.

HONOR (staff), "A Solution that's Working," *HONOR Digest* 6(7): 1–12, 1996 discusses the rise of Indian gaming with particular reference to Wisconsin.

Mining

Cultural Survival Quarterly, 25(1), Spring 2001. The entire issue is devoted to mining's impact on native peoples around the world, with several articles on North America. I drew heavily on the excellent account by Al Gedicks and Zoltán Grossman, "Native Resistance to Multinational Mining Corporations in Wisconsin," pp. 9–11.

Federal Recognition

Indian Report (newsletter of the Friends Committee on National Legislation, Washington, D.C.). Most of the Winter 2001 issue was devoted to the topic. I also depend on my subscription to the *Brothertown Quarterly Report.*

News from Indian Country (bimonthly newspaper; 7831 N. Grindstone Ave., Hayward, WI 54843-2052). Besides its own reporting and editorials, it publishes articles from other papers about U.S. and Canadian Indians, news about First Peoples from around the world, Indian columnists, film and book reviews, sports reports, and a regularly updated powwow directory for all of North America.

Internet

Indian Country, Milwaukee Public Museum: http://www.mpm.edu/wirp. This Web site provides general, regularly updated information and links to the various tribal and intertribal organizations' Web sites.

INDEX